Legendary Texians

Volume II

Joe Tom Davis

EAKIN PRESS
Austin, Texas

Davis, Joe Tom, 1942–
  Legendary Texians

  Bibliography: v. 2, p.
  Includes index.
  1. Texas — Biography. 2. Frontier and pioneer life — Texas. 3. Texas
— History. I. Title.
F385.D28 1985   976.4'009'92 [B]   84-18685
ISBN 0-89015-473-2 (v. 2)

FIRST EDITION
VOL. II

Copyright © 1985
By Joe Tom Davis

Published in the United States of America
By Eakin Press, P.O. Box 23066, Austin, Texas 78735

ISBN 0-89015-473-2

This book is dedicated to
my brother and sister,
Cecil Davis and
Shirley Davis Bonnot

Contents

I   **Brit Bailey and Strap Buckner:**   1
Legendary Characters of Early Texas

II   **Josiah Wilbarger:**   The Man Who   17
Survived His Scalping

III   **Pamelia Mann:**   She Did It Her Way   27

IV   **Gail Borden:**   A Texas Success Story   41

V   **The Saga of Cynthia Ann and**   68
Quanah Parker

VI   **L.H. McNelly:**   The Ranger Who Kept   103
on Coming

VII   **John Wesley Hardin:**   A Gunfighter and   127
His Times

VIII   **Roy Bean:**   Barroom Judge and Con Man   155

     Bibliography   175

     Index   181

About The Author

Joe Tom Davis is a fifth generation Texan; his maternal great-great-grandfather, George Lord, was a survivor of the Mier Expedition and the "Lottery of Death."

He attended public schools at Edna, Texas, where his interest in and love of Texas history was whetted by hearing Jackson County tales about the "Wild Man of the Navidad" and the ghost town of Texana, the Allen brothers' first choice for the site of the city of Houston.

Davis is a Navy veteran and earned two degrees from Sam Houston State University where he was elected to Alpha Chi, Who's Who, and received the James Ellison Kirkley Prize as outstanding social science student. After teaching at Sam Houston for two years, he joined the faculty of Wharton County Junior College in 1965 as an instructor of American and Texas history.

While teaching at the junior college, Davis has been elected to Outstanding Educators of America and is a leader in campus beautification efforts. He has a special interest in singing and is a choir member at First Baptist Church, El Campo. He often speaks to area study and service clubs and is a member of the Texas State Historical Association and the Texas Junior College Teachers Association. His first book, *Legendary Texians*, Volume I, was published by Eakin Press in the fall of 1982.

Acknowledgments

I could not have written this book without the assistance of my colleagues and friends. I am especially grateful for the support I received from Mrs. Patsy L. Norton, director of the J.M. Hodges Learning Center at Wharton County Junior College, and two members of her able staff. Assistant Director J.C. Hoke provided superior photographic reproductions while Mrs. Mildred Petrusek, the circulation technician, was always prompt in obtaining materials I needed through inter-library loans. Much of my reading and research was done in the Hodges Learning Center where an extensive collection of Texas history titles has been acquired since 1964 through the generosity of the Raymond Dickson Foundation and proceeds from the book, *The History of Wharton County*, by Annie Lee Williams.

I also wish to thank two members of the college English Department, Dr. Sandra Coats and Mr. R.L. Cowser, Jr., who advised me on matters of punctuation and usage. Mrs. Genelle Speer of Wharton, Texas, did excellent work in typing the manuscript in its final form. I am grateful to Mrs. George Rust, Jr., of Wharton for letting me use her genealogical records relating to Brit Bailey. For the illustrations in this book, I am indebted to Dr. W.G. McAlexander of Lake Jackson, Texas, and to the nine libraries, museums, societies, institutions, periodicals, and corporations which made available all of the photographs, portraits and maps I requested.

My greatest thanks and words of appreciation are due my late father and my mother, brother and sister; it was their steadfast support and encouragement which inspired me to write both this book and a companion volume.

Joe Tom Davis
Wharton County Junior College

Wharton, Texas

Introduction

In the first book of this series, I reviewed the lives of eight legendary Texians who belong on any listing of state notables. All were movers, shapers and super achievers who influenced their times; indeed, the names of Jane Long, Deaf Smith, David Burnet, William Barret Travis, Bigfoot Wallace, John Meusebach, Charles Goodnight and Shanghai Pierce conjure up larger-than-life images. All of them were "star" center stage players in the drama of Texas. In this volume, however, I have chosen to reach into the wings for a supporting cast of four colorful "characters," a half-breed Indian leader and his white mother, the founder of a dairy empire, a notorious gunman, a fearless Texas Ranger, and an ordinary pioneer who had an extraordinary experience. Their names may not be associated with the great events of Texas history but all are fascinating figures who enliven and enrich our state heritage.

The eccentric behavior of Brit Bailey, Strap Buckner, Pamelia Mann and Roy Bean made them legends in their own time. Bailey and Buckner were fiery-tempered brawlers who defied even *Empresario* Austin in asserting their rights. Brit fought for the pure fun of it while Strap, a giant of prodigious strength, was renowned for his amazing physical feats. Both were combatants in the first bloodletting between Texas and Mexico and Buckner was killed in the battle. After making a strange burial request, Brit died a few months later and locals say his ghost still roams Bailey's Prairie. Pamelia Mann broke the strictures of a "woman's place" in society to prosper as a tough acting and talking widow in a tough town. After facing down General Sam Houston during the Runaway Scrape, she became the notorious owner of the city of Houston's wildest house of ill repute, a madam with a long police record who remained socially prominent until her death. Judge Roy Bean was part buffoon and clown but through pure bluff and bluster, he used his combination courtroom–saloon to bring twenty years of law and order to a huge, wild frontier area. His court rulings and conduct made Judge Bean a tourist attraction for Southern Pacific passengers, who could expect a fleecing in his bar.

Quanah Parker is a noteworthy example of Indian material success in an Anglo world. There is an element of Greek tragedy in the story of his mother, Cynthia Ann Parker, a white girl captured by Indians who spent her adult life with the Comanches before being forcefully returned to "civilization," a melancholy existence, and a premature death. However, her tragic legacy turned to triumph through her loving, devoted half-breed son Quanah, who was destined to be the last recognized chief of the Comanches, a famous reservation leader and liaison with white officialdom, and the richest Indian in the United States when he died. His successful bridging of two alien, hostile cultures is symbolized today by annual family reunions of the Texas and Oklahoma Parker clans.

Gail Borden, Jr., the founder of a dairy empire, could be called a Texas-style Benjamin Franklin. Before assuring his fortune with the condensed milk patent, Gail was a schoolmaster, surveyor, land commissioner, editor, public servant, realtor, civic leader, Baptist lay leader, and inventor. He was Stephen F. Austin's most trusted friend and adviser, the Thomas Paine of the Texas Revolution, a surveyor who helped to lay out the city of Houston, and a city founder of Galveston. Although his first great experiment, the meat biscuit, left Borden deeply in debt, his faith in God and pure persistence led him to a greater discovery, condensing milk in a vacuum. Plant operations in Connecticut and New York made Gail a wealthy man but he retained a sentimental attachment for Texas where he spent his last winters and died.

L. H. McNelly and John Wesley Hardin were contemporaries on opposite sides of the law; an epic confrontation would surely have resulted if the paths of this fearless lawman and deadly gunfighter had crossed. McNelly was a Texas Ranger whose iron will, courage and daring inspired fanatical loyalty and devotion from his men. This small, frail, soft-spoken Ranger captain was dying of consumption when he took on the task of taming the Nueces Strip. In carrying out his own private war on Mexican cattle thieves, McNelly followed a brutal policy of terror, made law as he went, took no prisoners, and illegally invaded Mexico even as he defied the United States army and government. When his kind of law-enforcing proved politically embarrassing to the new Democratic state leadership, the desperately ill lawman was set adrift and died at age thirty-three. His potential adversary, John Wesley Hardin, was the greatest gunman in Western history; various estimates as to the number of his shooting victims range from twenty-seven to forty. In his autobiography this son of a Methodist preacher indicates no sense of remorse. In his view all his killings were right, principled acts; in fact, some were a sort of public service. A fugitive at age fifteen, Hardin used Gonzales County as a sanctuary until he was forced to leave Texas after killing a deputy sheriff. After being tracked down and captured in Pensacola, Florida, Wes became a reformed man while spending sixteen years in prison. However, he soon reverted to his base nature after his saintly wife's death and drifted to El Paso where he became a drinking, gambling town bully. After taking a prostitute as his woman, he died as he had lived, by the gun.

I have also chosen to include a "believe it or not" type of story. Josiah Wilbarger was a rugged pioneer who led an arduous, dangerous life but that could be said of scores of early Texas frontiersmen; indeed, he might have passed unnoticed in the stream of history but for an Indian attack. It is remarkable enough that he survived his scalping; even more extraordinary is the series of inexplicable coincidences that saved the wounded man's life. The apparition and dreams that led to Josiah's rescue were called a "marvel and a mystery" by his historian brother while Wilbarger's stepdaughter concluded that the chain of events surpassed earthly understanding. The reader is left to draw his own conclusions.

Writing this sampler has been a pleasurable experience for me. These were "real people" whose lives add spice and texture to the flavor and fabric of Texas history. I will, of course, take full responsibility for any errors made in the telling of their stories. I can only hope that my delight and enjoyment in writing this book will be conveyed to and shared by the reader.

I

Brit Bailey and Strap Buckner: Legendary Characters of Early Texas

Brit Bailey and Strap Buckner were original "characters" and prototypes of the independent, individualistic Texian. The two had much in common: Both were eccentric, fiery-tempered fighters; each was the first Anglo settler in his county; both were squatters in Austin's colony who defied the *empresario* and stayed on their land claims; each had a larger-than-life reputation; both took part in the first bloodletting between Texas and Mexico.

James Briton (Brit) Bailey, a descendant of the famed Robert Bruce of Scotland, was born in North Carolina on August 1, 1779. After living in Tennessee and Kentucky and serving as a navy captain in the War of 1812, he brought his wife Edith Smith and their six children to Texas and present Brazoria County in April 1821. Bailey was the first to build a cabin on the prairie named for him along the Brazos River. His home was built on Bennett's Ridge, the highest point of his land, and the Bailey plantation site is located today five miles west of Angleton along State Highway 35.

After Stephen F. Austin received permission from the Mexican Congress to bring three hundred Anglo families into Texas in April 1823, he disputed Bailey's prior

1

Drawings of Brit Bailey and Strap Buckner by Ann Brightwell,
Surfside, Texas.

Courtesy Brazosport Chamber of Commerce

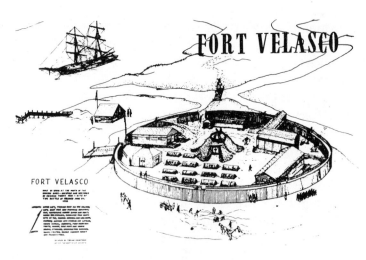

Fort Velasco
Courtesy Brazosport Chamber of Commerce

squatter claim to this prairie land. Since the land was within the limits of Austin's grant and had been assigned to Martin Varner, he wrote the following letter to Brit on October 3, 1823:

> You are hereby notified that you cannot be received as a settler in this colony, and that you will not be permitted to live nearer the Brazos River than the San Jacinto nor nearer the Colorado than the Guadaloupe.
> Sixty days are allowed you to remove your family and property.

On October 20 Austin reported to Governor Luciano Garcia that he was compelled to cause Bailey and four others to leave the colony since "... They are all men of infamous character and bad conduct, fugitives from the United States, one for having committed murder, the others for having counterfeited money ..." However, when Stephen went to Bailey's cabin to enforce the eviction order, he immediately retreated backwards prodded by Brit's rifle barrel. "Is it not a fact," Austin asked, "that you once served a term in the Kentucky penitentiary?" Brit retorted, " 'Taint *that* I'm ashamed of. It's the term I served in the Kentucky legislature which sets heavy on my conscience." He then proceeded to explain that while serving as a legislator, he had opposed the manufacture of so many banks which had ruined him and others. He had thus been tempted to the crime of forgery "to do that on a small scale, which they (the banks) had been doing on a great one." After "paying the forfeit," Bailey had stolen off to Texas to lead an honest and solitary life, wishing only to be left alone. A compromise was later reached, Varner received another grant, and Brit obtained a legal title to his league of land on July 7, 1824, to become one of Austin's "Old Three Hundred" colonists. He was thus able to live and die on his original claim.

Austin used Bailey's cabin when the settlers on the

lower Brazos met to take an oath of loyalty to the Mexican federal Constitution of 1824. At that meeting a company of militia was organized with Brit appointed as a lieutenant and he took part in the Battle of Jones Creek in September 1824. After the Karankawa Indians massacred some settlers, Austin authorized Captain Randal Jones and a party of twenty-three colonists to pursue them. Floating down the Brazos by canoes, Jones's men came upon thirty braves camped on the bank of a tributary of the San Bernard; today State Highway 36 crosses this Jones Creek between Brazoria and Freeport. When the colonists charged into the camp at daybreak, the melee resulted in a stalemate with both sides suffering losses before the Indians retreated across the San Bernard. Although the two never really got along, Austin also used Bailey to negotiate with the Indians; in such palavers, Brit's motto was, "Always be friendly, but never back up."

In April 1827 Stephen Nicholson and Peter Reynolds agreed to build Brit a frame house eighteen feet square with nine-foot galleries on each side. One-third of the cost, $220, was paid in cash with the balance due in good gentle cattle and hogs. By this time Bailey was becoming a successful cattleman and cotton grower and was expanding his acreage with land holdings extending from present Houston south to near the coast. His newfound status was confirmed in 1829 when Governor Jose Viesca commissioned him as a captain in the militia. An anonymous visitor to Texas in March 1831 visited Bailey's red-painted wooden house seven miles from Brazoria and described it as having a "very novel appearance for Texas." He was welcomed by the lame, limping Brit with the words, "Walk in, stranger." It seems that Bailey had just purchased a vicious mustang for twenty dollars; upon mounting he had been thrown over the horse's head and suffered a severe concussion. He told his guest that he had retaliated by slitting the critter's throat!

Brit was a "law unto himself," ruling the area with an iron hand and a long cracking whip. Awake or asleep, he was never beyond reach of his rifle, his "clenching argument." He would often turn heads by driving six yokes of oxen on some trips. Bailey richly deserved his reputation as a hard-drinking, hot-tempered, eccentric character. During one drinking binge he set fire to all the buildings on his property except the main house. He was also noted as an absolutely fearless brawler who was not to be crossed. When he went into Brazoria and found a fight in progress, he was likely to jump into the fracas by shouting, "Free fight, boys." On the way to town one day, he met one of the Austin men and said, "Prepare to fight!"; the two went at it until Bailey proclaimed, "That will do," then rode away. Another time when he discovered an Austin visiting one of his beautiful daughters at home, Brit reached for his rifle and ordered the young suitor to dance. Austin dutifully danced around solo-style with the irate father shooting at his feet until he could grab the rifle and announce, "Mr. Bailey, it is now your time to dance" — and Brit did. Once he was visited by a Methodist circuit preacher who needed a room for the night. Even the minister was forced to disrobe, get on the table, and dance "Juba," a dance or jig of Southern plantation slaves.

Brit's marital status was also a subject of controversy. It will be recalled that he brought his wife, Edith Smith Bailey, and their six children to Texas in 1821. However, an 1826 census of Austin's colony lists his wife's name as Nancy. In his Last Will and Testament, he left his property to his beloved Nancy and their two girls, Sarah and Margaret, while the three surviving children of Brit and Edith were entirely disinherited without cause. In 1838 Elizabeth Milburn and Mary Polley petitioned to have the will declared null and void, claiming that only they were legitimate children and that their father had only represented Nancy to be his wife. The plea was first denied, then the will was set aside in January 1839.

On June 26, 1832, Brit took part in the Battle of Velasco, the first bloodshed between Texas and Mexico. Trouble had been brewing ever since General Jose Mier y Teran conducted a political and military survey of Texas in 1828–1829. He discovered that hundreds of newcomer Anglo families were occupying land without governmental consent and that they vastly outnumbered the native Mexican population. The survey led him to an alarmist conclusion: The "North Americans" were taking Texas; Mexico must ask "now" or Texas "is lost forever." His recommendations were incorporated in the infamous state Colonization Law of 1830 which included a provision that customs collectors were to be sent to the Texas gulf ports. As a result of Teran's report, two Mexican forts were built, one on Trinity Bay at Anahuac and the other just below Velasco at the mouth of the Brazos River. Both fortifications provided a collecting agency for imports and controlled all river traffic. Colonel John Davis "Juan" Bradburn gave overall commands from Anahuac while Colonel Domingo de Ugartechea was in charge at Velasco.[1]

---

1. Fort Velasco, built in 1831, was located some 150 yards from both the riverbank and the Gulf shore. The outer circular wall was formed by parallel rows of logs six feet apart and filled in with sand, earth and shell. By standing on an embankment inside this wall, riflemen could fire over the top and expose only their heads to the enemy. In the center of the stockade was a higher rampart for a nine-pound swivel cannon protected by bulwarks. However, this artillery piece could not be depressed to fire at the ground near the fort walls. The main fort gate led to a dock on the riverfront and could be raised or lowered over a moat surrounding the stockade. Within the circular walls was a main building, customs office, cistern, barracks, stables, and a tent area.

The original plans for Fort Velasco, drawn in 1822 by Colonel Domingo de Ugartechea, were found in 1982 in the state archives in Austin. This important discovery was made by Jake Ivy, an archeologist at The University of Texas at San Antonio's Center for Archeological Research.

A showdown was triggered in June 1832 when Bradburn imprisoned William Barret Travis, Patrick Jack and Monroe Edwards at Anahuac, then reneged on a promise to Dr. Branch T. Archer to release them. After news of this incident spread through the Austin colony, a group of angry Anglo settlers went to Brazoria for two cannons where they also commandeered the schooner *Brazoria* at the wharf and were reinforced by "escort" militia companies from LaGrange, San Felipe, Columbia, Brazoria and Matagorda. The schooner then sailed down the Brazos bound for Anahuac, only to be turned back by Colonel Ugartechea and 150 troops at Fort Velasco. The rebuffed Texian militiamen then reassembled at William H. Wharton's Eagle Island Plantation (now Clute) where they collected arms, ammunition, supplies and organized into three companies, two of forty-seven men each and one composed of eighteen marines. John Austin, the senior officer present and mayor of Brazoria, was elected to command the first company with Henry S. Brown in charge of the second and William J. Russell commanding the *Brazoria* and the marine detachment. While the 112 colonists bivouacked at Eagle Island, they also constructed three-inch-thick cypress shields to serve as protection in storming Fort Velasco. It was said that four men were required to handle each of these barricades but Strap Buckner of Fayette County carried his own!

The plan of attack called for the schooner's two cannons and eighteen riflemen to fire harassing shots abreast of Fort Velasco while the other two companies approached by land from the north and east, using the cover of drift logs and the cypress palisades to creep under the fort's line of cannon fire. However, the battle was joined prematurely shortly before midnight on June 25 when one of Brown's men accidentally fired his musket and revealed the Texian presence to a Mexican lookout. As the conflict raged during the next eight hours, Austin's men found that enemy balls were riddling their cypress shields with holes; they then dug pits in the sand under the stockade walls where enemy fire could not reach them. Those Mexicans who dared expose themselves above the fort embankment were hit in the head, arms, wrists and hands by pinpoint Texian fire.

About 9:00 A.M. on June 26, a rainstorm forced the militiamen to withdraw from their positions; by this time, however, two-thirds of Ugartechea's men were dead or wounded and the Mexicans had exhausted their ammunition. At eleven o'clock that morning a white flag was hoisted over Fort Velasco and Colonel Ugartechea met and embraced his close friend, Captain Austin, under a flag of truce. The Mexican leader accepted surrender terms subject to two conditions: his officers could keep their sidearms and his command was to be furnished transportation to Matamoros. The *Brazoria* was thus free to sail to Anahuac with the two cannons, only to find the tense situation had been defused after Bradburn released his prisoners.

Two of Brit Bailey's sons, Smith and Gaines, were among the twenty-seven Texians wounded in the Battle of Velasco; the militia dead numbered seven while forty-two Mexican soldiers were killed with seventy being wounded. It was Brit who provided the best description of the battle in a letter he wrote on June 27, 1832. The final Mexican surrender occurred on June 29 in a camp at the mouth of the Brazos with Ugartechea's shattered command being allowed to peacefully leave Texas. Shortly thereafter General Jose Antonio Mexia arrived at the mouth of the Brazos with five gunboats. Ironically, since both he and the Texian militiamen were supporting Santa Anna in his struggle with President Bustamente, Mexia was allowed to take possession of Fort Velasco, then escorted to Brazoria for a fiesta in his honor.

Brit Bailey's eccentricity followed him to the grave. His will included a novel request ". . . to have my remains interd [*sic*] erect, with my face fronting the west . . ." In his last sickness and realizing that the end was near, he told his wife:

> I have never stooped to any man and when I am in my grave I don't want it said, 'There lies old Brit Bailey.' Bury me so that the world must say, 'There stands Bailey.' And bury me with my face to the setting sun. I have been all my life traveling westward and I want to face that way when I die.

After he died of cholera "fever" on December 6, 1832, an eight-feet deep, well-like hole was dug in the family graveyard, a pecan grove near his house, and Brit's pine box coffin was lowered feet first. Legend has it that he was buried standing with his old rifle by his side, powder horn on his shoulder, his favorite brace of pistols belted on with lead bullets at hand, and facing toward the West. No marking stone was placed so his exact burial site has been lost to time. When questioned as to his need for the firearms, Bailey explained, "You know I never yet was caught unarmed by Indian or wild beast. I . . . know not whom I might meet in another world. I wish to be prepared, as usual, for my enemies." Brit's huge servant, "Uncle Bubba," also tried to slip a jug of whiskey into his master's coffin but widow Nancy Bailey vetoed that and threw the spirits out the window; this was probably the first and only time she ever policed her husband's drinking habits. When a strange, eerie light later began to haunt Bailey's Prairie, Bubba had a simple explanation for the phenomenon: "Dat's why ole Marse Bailey he don't stan' easy in his grave. He's still out huntin' dat jug of whiskey." The faithful servant spent the rest of his life on the prairie and prophesied that the light would appear every seven years.

Ever since his death there have been tales of Brit Bailey's ghost reappearing to roam his land and of a mysterious light that haunts Bailey's Prairie. It seems that he first returned in human form. When John and Ann Raney Thomas bought the Bailey place a few years after his death, she noted that "it had a wild and gloomy appearance such as you often read of in enchanted places." On separate occasions in 1836 when first the wife and then the husband slept in Brit's bedroom, each was awakened in the dead of night by a cold sensation in the room; both were terrified to see the ghostly, floating figure of Bailey moving about the room and hovering near his death bed. Mrs. Thomas was also told that Brit's ghost stopped his former servant Jim from going home at night to visit his wife, who lived with a Bailey daughter a mile away. Jim, instead, always had to make the trip before sunset.

In the 1850s Brit's ghost was first seen in light form by Colonel Mordello Munson, who had a plantation home on the edge of Bailey's Prairie. After seeing a bright ball of fire some four miles away across the prairie, he chased it all night but never got closer than halfway to the light. In the fall of 1939, Robert and Joe Munson observed a floating, yellow-orange sphere the size of a basketball in the trees just off the prairie. Robert Munson saw Bailey's Light again in the same place in 1946, a couple sighted it along the highway in December 1953, and a woman who saw it in 1960 was too embarrassed to talk about the experience. In 1956 the lethal fumes of a gas well blowout tied up traffic for a week on Highway 35, prompting old-timers to surmise that the drilling had been close enough to disturb Brit's grave. The reader is left to ponder just when will be the next sighting of Brit Bailey's ghost roaming and searching for that long-lost jug of whiskey?

Aylett C. (Strap) Buckner, the son of Judge Aylett and Elizabeth Lewis Buckner of Louisa County, Virginia, was of Scotch and Irish ancestry. He was nicknamed "Strap" as he grew into a man huge in size, strength, appetite and thirst; his friends described him as being six feet, six inches tall and weighing about 250 pounds. Buckner was a veteran of three filibustering attempts to liberate Texas from Spanish rule. He first saw Texas in 1812 as a member of the Gutierrez–Magee expedition, came back with Francisco Xavier Mina in 1816, and then returned to stay with James Long's expedition in 1819. In fact, he later traveled to Matamoros, Mexico, seeking a land reward for services rendered Gutierrez and Mina.

Strap became the first permanent Anglo settler in present Fayette County in 1819 when he and partner Peter Powell built a cabin and made a squatter claim to land on a creek named for him on the west side of the Colorado River. In his *Letters from an Early Settler of Texas* (1853), W.B. Dewees later documented Buckner's squatter status by noting:

> We struck the Colorado at crossing of the old Bahia Road. No trace of civilization . . . We encamped on the river. A dog barked . . . We came upon a small log cabin on the west bank of the Colorado. Found therein two adventurers by the name of Buckner and Powell . . .

This log cabin near present LaGrange was built four years before Austin's land grant was confirmed and was fifty miles beyond the colony headquarters at San Felipe. Strap must have been an astute judge of land; twenty-six others in Austin's colony were later granted land either on Buckner's Creek or on the "waters of Buckner's Creek."

After Austin's empresario grant was confirmed in April 1823, he refused to recognize Strap as one of his colonists or to allow him title to the league of land including the forks of Hunney and Caney Creeks since Seth Ingram had already been awarded it. Instead, Buckner was granted title to one league and two labors of land in present Matagorda County as one of the "Old Three Hundred" in the summer of 1824. Violent quarrels with Austin over the proper location and amount of his land caused Strap to write a stinging protest letter to the empresario on April 20, 1825, in which he stated:

> I was one of the first men who built a cabin, the first man who had a plow stuck in the field. I have kept a house ever since I settled in your colony. I have never asked a man for the first cent for a man eating under my roof and have fed as many or more people, YOURSELF NOT EXCEPTED, and have not received the first cent. I have lost as much, and more of my property by Indian depredations than every other man on this river, or perhaps in the colony, with very few exceptions.

Buckner told Austin that he knew that lands were unequally divided, that he was not a simpleton and not blind, and that he would rather die than submit to such tyranny.

In 1825 Strap attempted to hold a convention to protest against Austin. His open defiance and refusal to move caused Austin to commission Andrew Rabb to arrest him for "disorderly and seditious conduct against the authorities of the government." This was a tall order indeed for Rabb, particularly since many colonists thought there was justice in Buckner's claim. In any case, Andrew suddenly got "sick" when he drew this assignment. Upon hearing of Austin's arrest order, the aroused Strap told the impresario to try it and see what happened! He literally stood by his guns, was neither arrested nor evicted, and stayed on his land. After being counseled by prominent colonists Jared E. Groce and John P. Cole on how to deal with Buckner, Austin found a graceful way out by writing Judge James Cummins that his "exceptionable" acts had been caused by a misunderstanding and that all was forgiven. This prompted the magnanimous squatter to offer to buy a thousand acres of the disputed land; it seems that he wanted to be sure of being buried under his own soil.

In the summer of 1824 Austin appointed Strap a militia captain to serve against the Indians and named him chairman of a committee of five to make a treaty with the thieving Waco and Tawakoni Indians. In drawing up the treaty, Buckner became the first Texian to set foot on their ancient council grounds below Waco. While returning from a Waco village, he was involved in an incident that gave him a reputation as a fiery-tempered duelist. It seems that his hungry companion, Thomas M. Duke, took some meat out of the pot while supper was still cooking, causing Buckner to acidly remark, "Duke, I wouldn't be such a damned dog." Thomas's reply so angered him that he challenged Duke to a duel using rifles at ten paces before both men simmered down.

After the Flowers and Cavanaugh families were murdered in 1826, Strap's party chased the guilty Karankawas, then surprised and killed thirty of them. The impressed Austin rewarded him with the rank of major to be in supreme command of a proposed massive offensive against the Indians. However, opposition from Mexican authorities caused the plan to be dropped. As late as 1831 Buckner led another attack on the Kronks at Live Oak Bayou. By then he was such a renowned foe that the Karankawas and Tonkawas called him the "Red Son of Blue Thunder." One Indian legend tells of his fighting the Devil toe-to-toe on a live oak hill all one day and night. Since his opponent constantly changed shape and size, Strap was placed at a competitive disadvantage so managed no better than a draw in the brawl before leaving the area for three months to recuperate. According to the legend the live oak hill was leveled to a treeless plain by the epic fight.

A census of March 1826 listed Buckner as a single man with four servants and one slave. Because of his past difficulties with Austin, Benjamin Edwards tried unsuccessfully to recruit him for service in the abortive Fredonian Rebellion at Nacogdoches that December; Stray instead signed resolutions protesting the uprising. Eventually he and Austin became good friends with Buckner even offering advice on how to collect debts by 1829. Further evidence of his transformation to a model citizen is revealed in the following letter to Austin:

> Agreeable to your request I have informed the people of your cuming [*sic*] with the Priest to christen and marry them. I am informed there will be numbers who will collect at Mrs. Williams for that purpose for they are now making preparations against your arrival. You will do me the pleasure to call. I shall try to make things as agreeable to you and Mr. Baladon [*sic*, Muldoon] as possible.

A red-haired giant of prodigious strength, Buckner was later ranked by *Harper's Magazine* as the equal of the legendary Paul Bunyan. Tales abound of his extraordinary physical feats. For example, he had a playful habit of personally welcoming each new colonist with a forceful and often incapacitating thump on the back. Strap would knock men down for no apparent reason except that he "felt compelled to do so." He would break into a circle of men and bowl them over one at a time with his massive shoulder; if anyone was injured, Buckner would tenderly nurse the casualty in his own home. It was said that he could knock a yearling dead with a bare fist. He developed a reputation as a mighty hunter, one who disdained the use of such "sissy" weapons as rifle or pistol; instead, he used his bare fists or a tomahawk, a chunk of scrap iron tied to a hickory handle, as he stalked wild game. A Karankawa warrior claimed that he once saw Strap stop a wildcat in midair with one mighty swing.

The most widespread Buckner tale concerns "Noche," a huge black killer bull with a six-foot horn spread that had terrorized Fayette County settlers. When they met to decide what collective action to take, Strap proclaimed, "I'll get him with my bare hands." After first being assured of a large audience, Buckner approached the bull armed only with a red blanket. The enraged beast raised his tail high, pawed the earth and bellowed, then charged while Strap also pawed the ground and roared even louder. Just as the crazed animal lunged, Buckner shot out his huge bare fist and made crunching contact; the bull staggered with blood pouring from its nostrils, then dropped and lay there for an hour. Noche finally wobbled off, never to be seen in those parts again.

The paths of Strap Buckner and Brit Bailey crossed in the twilight of their lives. In the summer of 1832 Captain Buckner drew up a will, then led a militia company of twenty men from Fayette County as part of the Texian assault on the Mexican coastal fort at Velasco. During the attack a Mexican bullet splintered Buckner's cypress shield and a wooden fragment pierced his head, causing instant death. His Mexican boy servant Jose also died in the Battle of Velasco, a fight that Brit Bailey survived. Fact and fiction truly blend in recounting the exploits of these two remarkable Texians; of such men are legends made.

Josiah and Margaret Wilbarger, around 1830
Courtesy Bastrop County Historical Society

II

Josiah Wilbarger:
The Man Who Survived His Scalping

One of the most incredible dramas in Texas history unfolded near present Austin in the summer of 1833. When Josiah Wilbarger's stepdaughter, Miss Fenora Chambers, was interviewed years later by the *Dallas Morning News*, she summed up the chain of events by concluding that "it is just one of those things which we do not expect to understand on this earth." In 1889 Josiah's brother, John Wesley, wrote *Indian Depredations in Texas* and made the following observation about the series of incidents:

> We leave to those more learned the task of explaining the strange coincidence of the visions of Wilbarger and Mrs. Hornsby. It must remain a marvel and a mystery. Such things are not accidents; they tell us of a spirit world and of a God who "moves in a mysterious way his wonders to perform."

These awestruck relatives were describing a legendary tale about a rugged frontiersman who survived his scalping and lived because of his unearthly vision and a pioneer woman's inexplicable dreams.

Josiah Wilbarger, the eldest of eight children, was born in Bourbon County, Kentucky, in September 1801.

17

Old photograph of Wilbarger house
Courtesy Bastrop County Historical Society

Recent photograph of Wilbarger house
Courtesy Bastrop County Historical Society

The family was "Dutch" and the highest ideal of his father John was to educate his sons in English rather than the German language that "had made it very hard and awkward for him in his social and business relations with his fellowmen in a new country." John Wilbarger was a farmer but sent sons Josiah, Mathias, and John Wesley to school in Frankfort, a place where Indian attacks were an ever-present danger. While a student there Josiah was taught to survey and mold bullets and his knowledge of military tactics won him the title of "colonel."

The Wilbarger family moved to Pike County, Missouri, when Josiah was age twenty-two. There he met one of Stephen F. Austin's agents and in 1827 signed on as one of the Kentucky–Missouri members of Austin's second colony on the upper Colorado River in Texas. After he married Margaret Baker that September, the newlyweds traveled by boat from St. Louis to New Orleans to Matagorda, arriving on the Texas coast in December 1827. At first Josiah taught there and then at LaGrange for a year. He then turned to surveying and in March 1830 located his headright at the mouth of Wilbarger Creek along a bend in the Colorado. His farm was located about ten miles above present Bastrop with the nearest neighbor being some seventy-five miles down river; in fact, he was the first and outside settler until July 1832. After building a log stockade Wilbarger brought Margaret and his oldest son John there to live. When Indians observed his wife coolly molding bullets and reloading guns during an attack, they dubbed her the "Brave Squaw." Josiah came to own many tracts of land and accumulated a trunkload of silver coins through trading. In early 1832 he took his family to New Orleans where he exchanged the specie for greenbacks and purchased household supplies. Upon their return to Texas, both husband and wife had packed money belts strapped to their bodies.

Josiah's friend and first neighbor, Reuben Hornsby,

was born near present Rome, Georgia, in January 1793. He married Sarah Morrison, a dainty, black-haired lass of pure Scotch descent, at her Vicksburg, Mississippi, plantation home in the fall of 1816. After the couple had a family of seven boys and one girl, Reuben was struck by "pioneer fever" and decided to come to Texas. Mrs. Hornsby, a cultured woman who sang Highland ballads with a sweet soprano voice, insisted on bringing her books and music on the ox-wagon journey. In February 1830 the family reached Texas and joined Austin's Little Colony at Mina (Bastrop) where Reuben became a surveyor. After selecting his own land at a bend of the Colorado nine miles below Austin, he built a double-log cabin there in July 1832. His beautiful tract stretched eastward over a level valley three miles wide; the wild rye growing there resembled a huge green wheat field. Hornsby thought the soil contained the chemical properties to sustain four generations without extra fertilizer, a calculation which proved to be true; in fact, the Hornsbys had the first corn and wheat harvests in present Travis County in 1832.

Sarah was a devout Baptist so their home and a big oak tree in the yard became the site of the first Baptist church services in the county. The Hornsbys were also noted for their hospitality; their home was a stopping place for single young men who brought news from the States *and* provided additional protection. Since the two families were the "outside settlers" in the area, the Hornsbys and Wilbargers became close friends. They were also joined by a common bond of danger since this frontier region was on the extreme fringe of Comanche country.

In early August 1833, Josiah stopped at Hornsby's Bend to join a surveying party of four men scouting for headrights to the northwest. Christian and Strother were Austin colony settlers while Haynie and Standifer were recent arrivals from Missouri looking for their own land.

When the group reached Walnut Creek, they spotted and hailed an Indian, who refused to parley and fled toward the cedar-covered hills. At noon the surveying party stopped at Pecan Springs, four miles east of what is now the capital city, to eat a lunch of cornpone and jerky. Wilbarger, Christian and Strother unsaddled their horses and hobbled them to graze while the other two men merely staked their saddled mounts. While they were eating, the group was suddenly attacked by Comanche Indians on foot. After first running to some scant cover offered by small trees, Haynie and Standifer broke for their saddled horses and raced away toward the safety of Hornsby's house where they later recalled looking back to see Josiah fall with "about fifty Indians around him."

During the attack Strother and Christian were mortally wounded and had their throats slit while Wilbarger received arrow wounds in both legs and a flesh wound in a hip. Just when he stood up to shout for help from the two fleeing horsemen, Josiah took a ball from the rear through the center of his neck that came out under his chin. When the Comanches saw the hole, they assumed he had died from a broken neck and stripped off his clothes. As the victim later told it, this shot only "creased" or temporarily paralyzed him, leaving Josiah conscious but unable to move, near-blind from shock, numbed and feeling no pain. Thus he knew but did not flinch when a warrior cut and tore seven pieces of scalp from his head, each one about the size of a dollar; Wilbarger later said that the ripping noise "sounded like the pealing of loud, distant thunder." When he regained consciousness, he heard loud wails and screams of grief, anguish and anger. Those Indians nearby were called away due to the death of a brave; in fact, the yells saved his life since the warriors were thus distracted and did him no further harm.

The sun was halfway down when he was awakened by a terrible thirst and awful stabs of pain. Still bleeding and with dried blood caking his entire body, Wilbarger crawled some three hundred yards to the camp water hole, a shallow pool, where he drank and then lay in the water an hour to soothe his raging fever. It would be difficult to even imagine the searing pain he must have felt when the water touched his exposed skull. After becoming chilled and numb, he pulled himself out on dry land and placed his only piece of clothing, a sock, on his throbbing head, then fell into a deep sleep. It was near nightfall when Josiah awoke to find green blowflies buzzing around his head and laying eggs in his wounds; he could even feel the maggots crawling in his naked flesh. After drinking more water and finding snails to eat, he decided to try to crawl the six miles to the Hornsby house. He traveled only six hundred yards before total exhaustion forced Wilbarger to sit down and prop himself against the trunk of a large post oak tree. The wounded, naked man was awakened shortly after midnight by the intense cold. At first he noticed only the bright stars and the sound of barking coyotes and hooting owls. But then Josiah had a remarkable vision: he suddenly saw the distinct figure of his sister, Mrs. Margaret Clifton, who lived more than seven hundred miles away at Florisant, Missouri. Standing near her brother, this apparition calmly said, "Brother Josiah, you are too weak to go by yourself. Remain here and friends will come to take care of you before the setting of the sun." Then he saw Margaret drift away in the direction of Hornsby's house.

Shortly thereafter Mrs. Sarah Hornsby suddenly awoke from a deep sleep, shook her husband, and cried out, "Wilbarger is not dead. I saw him in a dream. He sits naked under a large post oak tree, covered with blood from wounds, scalped. But he is not dead. I saw him plainly." Reuben was able to calm his wife and get her back to sleep but she awoke again about three o'clock, sprang from the bed and cried, "I saw him again!" This time her husband could not pacify her; Sarah Hornsby dressed, aroused all the men, and had their coffee and breakfast made by daybreak. One of the awakened men who had escaped the ambush insisted that he had seen Wilbarger shot down and scalped. When he proclaimed that Indians never left a victim breathing, Mrs. Hornsby replied that *she* had the *last* look at Wilbarger, that he was alive, and that the rescue party must go at once. When daylight came and Reuben Hornsby and the rescue party prepared to ride out, his wife insisted that they take three sheets, two for burying Christian and Strother and one to wrap around Wilbarger. She also filled a Mexican gourd with milk since Josiah would be hungry.

When the rescue party reached the campsite where the Indians had attacked the day before, they quickly found the two naked, mutilated corpses of Strother and Christian. Two sheets were left over the bodies and they were buried the next day. The group also discovered the body of a warrior shot through the head; he had been wrapped in a buffalo hide and left in a dense thicket. Nearby they found a scalp hanging from a tree. After a prolonged search late into the afternoon, one of the party, Joseph Rogers, spotted a sunburned, blood-caked figure under a big post oak tree. Assumming that he had seen a wounded Indian, Rogers shouted, "Here they are, boys," and raised his gun to fire. At that instant the figure struggled to his feet, raised his hands and moaned, "Don't shoot, boys, it is Wilbarger." He was gently lifted into the saddle of Rogers's horse with Hornsby's lighter, sixteen-year-old son William holding him from behind, and with the sheet wrapped around him. When the search party reached the Hornsby cabin after a slow ride, Sarah was ready for her patient and said simply, "I knew you would bring him." She had already prepared a bed, warm water to cleanse his wounds, wheat bread poultices, and bear's oil to dress Josiah's head.

For days Sarah nursed him with roots and herbs while the wounded man talked deliriously of his sister

Margaret. After Mrs. Hornsby finally told him of her two dreams, the two concluded that it must have been Margaret telling her to send the men. Six weeks later they decided to write Mrs. Clifton but then a letter arrived from Missouri: Josiah Wilbarger learned that his sister had died the day *before* he was wounded and that her body was in the grave at the very hour of his vision.

Eventually Josiah was able to leave Hornsby's place on a sled drawn by plodding horses; he could not stand the motion of a wagon ride. When even the bumpy sled ride became too painful, some friends took the ropes in hand and carried him the rest of the way home. Although he recovered from his ordeal to live another twelve active years, the skin never grew entirely over a small place in the middle of the old scalp wound and the skull bone became diseased, leaving the brain exposed. During his waking hours, even at the dinner table, Wilbarger always wore a silk cap over the open sore and scarred scalp while he put on a nightcap at bedtime. The skull caps were made from his wife's expensive silk wedding dress, which provided enough material to last for years. His outdoor life was limited by the need to protect his skull from heat and cold but Josiah still managed to build one of the first grist mills in present Bastrop County and partially completed a belted and pulley-type generator motor. He was also a student of the *Bible* and Shakespeare and taught area children the three "R's" by word of mouth. Wilbarger was farming again by 1836 and contributed to the Revolutionary cause by supplying meat and provisions to the Texas army.

His death was hastened when Josiah accidentally bumped his head on a low door frame in the cotton gin house. Inflammation set in the scalp bone despite the best efforts of his physician, Dr. Anderson, who could only try to ease the pain and suffering. After requesting that a locust tree be planted at his grave, Wilbarger's last words were, "That is as far as I can go . . ." He died at home in Bastrop on April 11, 1845, and was buried in Fairview Cemetery. His last home, a two-story porticoed frame house built in 1842, still stands and has been occupied by Josiah's descendents ever since. He was survived by his wife and five children; widow Margaret later married Talbert C. Chambers. After his death she lived to a ripe old age and was buried beside her first husband. In 1858 Wilbarger County was created and named for Josiah and his brother Mathias. Another brother, John Wesley, a Methodist minister, came to Texas from Missouri in 1837 and wrote a classic book, *Indian Depredations in Texas*, in 1889. On April 21, 1932, the bodies of Josiah Wilbarger and his wife were reinterred in the State Cemetery at Austin.

Their eldest son, John L., was also destined to die at the hands of Indians. He was born on November 29, 1829, at Matagorda but grew up in Bastrop County where he gained a reputation as a daring, skilled Indian fighter. While still in his teens, John joined a Ranger company led by Colonel John S. "Rip" Ford. In the summer of 1850 young Wilbarger took a lengthy furlough to visit his mother and family at Bastrop. He then returned to duty with two others named Neal and Sullivan, intending to join their unit which was patrolling between San Antonio and the Rio Grande. On August 20 a large Indian war party discovered the three Rangers on an open prairie near San Patricio. His two companions were downed by the first volley but John spurred his horse and fled for his life. After a two-mile chase, the lathered mount broke down, leaving Wilbarger on foot and armed with a gun and two six-shooters. In the desperate fight that ensued, he killed several savages before being literally cut to pieces. When his mutilated body was found by a search party, pools of blood covered the scarred earth of the battle site. John was given a decent burial on the spot but years later his brother Harvey removed the remains to near his father's grave in Fairview Cemetery.

This story would not be complete without further reference to Sarah Hornsby, who was to have her own tragic encounters with the Indians. Once when all the menfolk were gone from Hornsby's Bend, she dressed like a man and paraded about with a rifle as a ruse to scare off lurking savages. In 1836 the first two graves in the Hornsby Cemetery were filled by two young soldiers detailed by the Texas army to protect the settlers; they were caught off-guard while hoeing corn and butchered by Indians as Sarah watched helplessly from her cabin door. Her own son Daniel was killed in a Comanche attack in 1845. Reuben eventually built his wife a beautiful new home from handsawed lumber with a distinctive feature being an attic with portholes on all four sides for detecting and firing on Indians; thus the place was called Hornsby's Fort. The independent Sarah made a horseback visit to her Vicksburg home in 1849, accompanied only by her son Joseph and some slaves. She died at her Hornsby's Bend home on April 20, 1862, bringing the curtain down on one of the great dramas in Texas history.

III

Pamelia Mann:
She Did It Her Way

Pamelia Mann lived only six of her years in Texas, yet in that brief time she became a legendary figure by breaking out of the confines of a "woman's place" in society. She first became notorious as the woman who defied General Houston and the Texas army during the Runaway Scrape; she then became well-known throughout the Republic of Texas as the owner of the young city of Houston's wildest bawdy house. She used language seldom heard from a lady and compiled a long police record — but still achieved a position of social prominence; she was a tough-fibered widow who became financially secure in a tough town.

This free-spirited woman and her two sons, Flournoy Hunt and Sam Allen, came to Texas in 1834 with her husband, Marshall Mann. Sailing from New Orleans by schooner, they ran the Mexican blockade at Galveston Island and landed at Harrisburg. The Manns soon moved northwest and settled on a Brazos River farm in Sterling C. Robertson's colony, which was second in size only to Austin's colony with *Empresario* Robertson bringing in more than six hundred families before the Texas Revolution. Today there is a state marker twelve miles west of

Hearne which locates the site of the colony capital town of Nashville.

Pamelia was in a feisty mood when she first surfaced in the historical records. O.M. Addison, a Methodist minister, notes in his unpublished reminiscences that his father moved to Robertson's colony in 1835, bringing two large ox-drawn wagons. After one of the teamsters tore down a fence blocking the trail and then drove through an enclosure surrounding a house, the second wagon started to repeat the shortcut; suddenly a young man appeared with musket in hand and ordered the driver to turn back. According to Reverend Addison,

> At this juncture, Mrs. Mann, standing in the doorway of the house near by, cried out to the young man in strong, angry tones: 'Shoot him down, Nimrod! Shoot him down! Blow his brains out!' (Nimrod was her son, Flournoy Hunt.)
>
> ... the young man still hesitated, when my father taken advantage of the pause, interposed, and the matter was pacified by the wagons going around.

Mrs. Mann's most famous escapade occurred during the Texas Revolution. After the fall of the Alamo to Santa Anna's forces, General Sam Houston burned Gonzales and led a six-week retreat eastward with 374 men. News of his movement triggered the "Runaway Scrape," a widespread panic and civilian flight to keep ahead of the advancing Mexican army. When Houston reached San Felipe he retreated up the Brazos River and camped on the west bank for twelve days at Leonard Groce's Bernardo plantation. While there he gained reinforcements, drilled his army, and received two six-pound cannons, the "Twin Sisters," as a gift from the people of Cincinnati, Ohio.

Pamelia Mann was one of many civilian refugees who made her way to Bernardo plantation, bringing two large freight wagons pulled by eight oxen from the abandoned family farm. Robert Coleman, one of Houston's un-

The executive mansion at Houston
Courtesy Harris County Heritage Society

Capitol Hotel, Houston, 1837
Courtesy Harris County Heritage Society

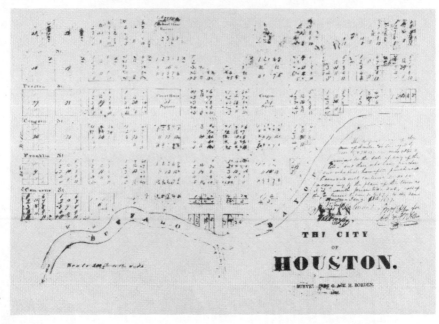

Earliest map of Houston, 1836
Courtesy Harris County Heritage Society

friendly aides, later claimed that she and the general
were soon on very cordial terms. According to Coleman's
unsubstantiated account, some soldiers entered Houston's tent unannounced to find Sam lying down with his
head in Mrs. Mann's lap while she combed his hair; the
startled Pamelia exclaimed, "Boys, you nearly made me
drive the comb into the general's head!" Houston later
asked if he could borrow her spare yoke of draft oxen to
pull his cannons through the flooded, boggy countryside.
She gave conditional approval by replying, "General, if
you are going to follow the Nacogdoches road, you can
have my oxen. But if you turn off and go the road to Harrisburg, you can't have them. I want them myself." Houston satisfied her by saying, "Well, I am going the Nacogdoches road," but he did not say *how far* he was going on
it. He then turned the animals over to Captain Conrad
Rohrer, the wagonmaster who was commandeering oxen,
mules and horses for the army's transportation.

On April 12, 1836, General Houston crossed the Brazos River on the steamboat *Yellowstone*. Heavy rainfall slowed his advance but by nightfall on April 16 he reached a major crossroads: Harrisburg and a certain battle with Santa Anna was to the right fork while Nacogdoches and asylum in the United States was to the left. The "Which Way Tree" and the site of this crossroads is located today eight miles east of Tomball. The small drum and fifer corps at the head of Houston's army headed to the right fork and Houston followed with the order, "Columns right." He did, however, order Wylie Martin to escort and protect the families who took the left fork in their flight toward the Sabine River. The Texas army was now on a fifty-five mile forced march to Harrisburg and the Battle of San Jacinto.

Twelve miles on toward Harrisburg, the screaming and cursing Pamelia caught up with the army to confront General Houston. According to two eyewitnesses, she was carrying two pistols, a long bowie knife, and a whip. Wagonmaster Rohrer ignored her protests, referred her to the general, and urged her oxen on with his bullhorn voice and colorful language. When she reached Houston, Mrs. Mann shouted, "General, you told me a damned lie. You said you was agoin' to Nacogdoches. Sir, I want my oxen." He retorted, "Madam, don't irritate me," and proceeded to explain that he must have the oxen to move the cannons. Pamelia then unleashed a stream of oaths the likes of which Houston, himself an expert in the art of swearing, had never heard. Finally he threw up his arms in despair and said, "Take them, my dear woman, for God Almighty's sake, take them!"

R.H. Hunter, a witness to the confrontation, wrote in his diary that

> She turned a round to oxen and jumpt down with knife & cut the raw hide tug that the chane was tied with, the log chane was brokd . . ., no body said a word, she jumpt on her horse with whip in hand, & way she went in a lope with her oxen.

A different version came from eyewitness S. F. Sparks, who wrote that Mrs. Mann:

> . . . drew a pistol and rode up by the side of the team and said, 'Wo!' The team stopped. Houston ordered the driver to drive on. The driver fell in the water and said, 'Oh, Lord, I'm shot!' The woman unhitched the oxen and drove them off. We called this Houston's defeat.

When Captain Rohrer protested that he could not get along without the oxen, the ever-gallant Houston replied that they would have to get along as best as they could; then in boot-top mud and slush, the general put his shoulder to the wheel of the cannon wagon and asked for volunteers to help him push. R. H. Hunter notes that "8 or 10 men more lade holt, out she come, & on we went." As Pamelia rode off, Wagonmaster Rohrer requested permission to overtake her and try to recover the oxen. Houston gave his approval to the attempt with the parting warning, "Captain . . . that woman will bite." By then Rohrer was some distance away when he defiantly shouted back, "Damn her biting!" Six miles farther on, the crestfallen captain caught up with the marching army when they camped after nightfall; he had no oxen and his shirt was torn to shreds. After Rohrer lamely explained that "she would not let me have them," a camp joke spread to the effect that Mrs. Mann had wanted his shirt for baby rags while the men called the whole episode "Houston's defeat."

The paths of Sam Houston and Pamelia Mann soon crossed again in more pleasant circumstances. On November 30, 1836, the First Congress of the Republic of Texas chose the new city of Houston as the capital over fifteen competitors. Colonel Benjamin Fort Smith, a former Indian fighter and agent, slave trader, and veteran of San Jacinto, moved from Brazoria County to become one of Houston's first residents. In early 1837 he hauled in logs from the forest and built the city's first hotel on two lots at the northeast corner of Congress and Milam streets. Smith operated it a short time, then sold the establishment to Mrs. Mann on June 8, 1837. After moving from burned-out Harrisburg, the new proprietor renamed the place the Mansion House. Pamelia quickly made this combination tavern and brothel the capital's leading hotel; in fact, it was located only a short distance from both the Capitol and the Executive Mansion.

The Mansion House was described as "a commodious, two-storied, plastered building with porches." The parlour was furnished with a sofa, a cherry center table, an eight-day clock, six chairs and a pair of spittoons. The dining room contained two long tables set with china and German silver cutlery; diners could order coffee, tea, hard liquor or wine from black serving girls. The second floor contained three rooms with each having washstands, mirrors and beds. At least one of the rooms was furnished dormitory-style with double and single beds. In writing about Pamelia Mann in the *Southwest Review* (Summer, 1935), William Ransom Hogan described her hotel thusly:

> The Mansion House was no shrine of gourmets, but sensitive palates were rare in that day of five- to fifteen-minute meals. When it was desired, feminine companionship of a robust and none too virtuous nature must be provided. Boarding houses, often dignified with the name of hotels, were set up to care for this portion of the male population which had to exist without benefit of wifely solicitude. In this last respect, Mrs. Mann and her 'girls' achieved a satisfying success.

It was, no doubt, the "satisfying success" of the Mansion House that inspired two Houston morals ordinances. A city law of 1840 provided a fine of at least fifty dollars and a jail term up to thirty days for any woman committing lewd acts or exhibiting herself in a public place in a style "not usual for respectable females;" the law also decreed that brothels in the city limits could not be within two squares of a family residence. In order to insure good behavior, an 1841 ordinance required a twenty-dollar bond for a "female of ill fame" found in a public place after 8:00 P.M.

On April 21, 1837, the city of Houston hosted the first San Jacinto Day Ball in the still unfinished Carlos Saloon. President Houston was in attendance and at midnight the guests adjourned to the uncompleted Mansion House for supper. There they feasted on deer, quail and ducks brought in by hunters and Indians, then washed the repast down with a wide choice of wines imported from New Orleans. At the conclusion of the meal, General Thomas J. Rusk, resplendent in his military dress uniform, stood and offered the toast, "Houston, with all thy faults I love thee still!" The beaming Sam Houston joined in drinking the toast. There had been hard feelings between the two for more than a year, starting when Rusk as interim Secretary of War had criticized Houston's strategy of retreating rather than standing to fight Santa Anna's army. Their feud had continued even after the Battle of San Jacinto but this toast at the Mansion House seemed to patch up these past differences.

According to legend, Susanna Dickinson, the sole Anglo adult survivor of the Alamo assault, stayed at the Mansion House for a time. It was said that she ran with a fast crowd in Houston and that Pamelia Mann was a girl friend. Another frequent visitor of note at the Mansion House was the lovelorn President Houston, who was drunk much of the time and writing daily letters to Miss Anna Raguet, his teenage girl friend at Nacogdoches. At the time, he and Army Surgeon-General Dr. Ashbel Smith were sharing bachelor quarters in the Executive Mansion, which was actually a two-room shack with dirt floors and liquor kegs, barrels, boxes and spare cots for furniture. One of Dr. Smith's duties was to hold a tight rein on Sam's drinking but the two would often walk the short distance to Mrs. Mann's place to unwind and sample its assorted pleasures.[1]

It was common for several men to share the same room in the Mansion House. In 1837 the famous Laurens–Goodrich duel resulted because two such roommates proved to be less than congenial. This affair of honor came about after Dr. Benjamin Goodrich, a dashing Mississippian, falsely accused young Mr. Laurens of stealing a thousand dollar bill during the night. After the

---

1. Ashbel Smith was born on August 13, 1805, at Hartford, Connecticut. At age nineteen he graduated from Yale University with a Phi Beta Kappa key and fluent in Latin and French; in 1828 he received a degree from Yale Medical College. After practicing at Salisbury, North Carolina, for three years, Smith traveled to France for further study in October 1831. Upon his return to Salisbury the next year, he became involved in politics as editor of the *Western Carolinian.* Dr. Smith emigrated to the Republic of Texas in 1837, was appointed surgeon-general of the Texas army, and became a drinking partner, close friend, and the personal physician of President Sam Houston. In fact, before Ashbel retired to a Galveston practice in 1838, he was moved to defend Houston's health and state of mind to a New Orleans newspaper. When Sam married Margaret Lea at Marion, Alabama, in May 1840, Smith was to be his best man but could not afford the trip. Years later Margaret discovered a tumor in her breast but refused to allow a local doctor to examine her. In March 1847 the dutiful Dr. Smith traveled from Galveston to her Grand Cane home and removed the growth; during the incision teetotaler Margaret bit on a silver coin rather than resort to whiskey as an anesthesia! The absent Senator Houston credited Ashbel with saving his wife's life. When Sam lay dying of pneumonia at Huntsville in July 1863, Smith traveled to his bedside to confirm the diagnosis and dolefully admit there was nothing he could do.

From 1842 until 1844 Dr. Smith was the Texas chargé d'affaires to both England and France, then was called home to be Anson Jones's Secretary of State. During the Civil War he was appointed a brevet brigadier general charged with defending Matagorda peninsula and Galveston Island. Smith also served three terms in the state legislature, was president of the Board of Regents of The University of Texas, and a founder of the Texas Medical Association and the Texas Medical College and Hospital at Galveston. A lifelong-but-amorous bachelor, he died on January 21, 1886, at Evergreen plantation, his home on Galveston Bay, and was buried in the State Cemetery at Austin.

hapless Laurens was killed in the duel, Marcus Cicero Stanley, another bedfeellow and the real culprit, was caught trying to cash the bill in New Orleans. An aroused citizenry forced Goodrich to leave Houston but he wrote back to Dr. Ashbel Smith, asking that he supervise his Negroes. The duelist's respect for his former landlady is revealed in the following passage of the letter:

> Sam, (my negro body servant) is also under your charge. He says he will pay to you Seven Dollars Pr. Week, and the money must be paid without fail, if he does fail to do so, hire him to the most Sever. Master (say Mrs. Man.) *She will train him.*

In his book, *Texian Emigrant* (1840), Edward Stiff describes Mrs. Mann as "a most notorious character" and claims that on two different occasions, she faced down the Houston police force. After a local doctor charged that Pamelia had stolen his trunk, the city constable arrived at the Mansion House with a warrant for her arrest. After he was "out-tongued" and ejected, the officer returned with half a dozen reinforcements. According to Stiff, "The Madam . . . called to aid a band of renegades which she retains in her service, and emphatically declared that her house shall inherit the fame of Goliad if the invading army did not immediately beat a retreat." The next thing Stiff knew, some husky constables were scampering back across the common.

Some local residents then decided "to test the moral honesty" of the police with a setup job: they allowed Pamelia to steal another trunk containing some very valuable contents. She was arrested in her office by the sheriff, who decided to carry out his investigation in her hotel; law officers and numerous spectators could thus combine business with some "delicious refreshments." Although the prosecutor proved her guilt, he left the hotel during a brief recess and was locked out upon his return while a "small garrison" inside held the whole party hostage until they promised to leave quietly and forget the whole matter.

The Mansion House was notorious for its rowdy guests but Mrs. Mann, whose husband died in 1838, had a reputation for controlling brawls, duels and police raids. When the hotel opened, the city of Houston had more than one hundred finished houses and some 1,500 residents, many of whom were gamblers, drifters or speculators. The capital was a rough place; it was common to see men walking the streets with up to four pistols and a bowie knife belted around. Pamelia was known to her clientele as an expert at firearms, knives, horseback riding, and profanity and was said to have "fought everyone except the Indians." The records of Harrisburg (now Harris) County show that she developed an extensive police record of her own from 1836 until 1840. During this period she was involved in more litigation and prosecuted for more different crimes than any man: the charges included counterfeiting, fornication, larceny and assault with intent to kill.

In 1839, Pamelia had her closest call when a forged document caused her to stand trial for her life. Due to a rash of forged land titles, the first Congress of the Republic of Texas had passed a law making forgery a capital offense. Back in 1836 a Mr. Hardy had loaned Mrs. Mann money to finance a boardinghouse for the delegates meeting in convention at Washington-on-the-Brazos. When he died the Widow Hardy requested repayment of the loan and Pamelia courted disaster by forging a receipt indicating that she had already repaid four hundred dollars of the debt. After the alert widow filed charges, a Harris County jury found Mrs. Mann guilty of forgery on May 22, 1839, and District Judge B.C. Franklin sentenced her to be "hanged by the neck till she is dead" on June 27. She was led back to the filthy, foul-smelling, cramped, two-cell Houston jail to await her execution but was there only one day before the jury recommended to

President Mirabeau B. Lamar that she be treated with leniency. Their petition stated:

> ... That considering the peculiar situation of the accused, being a female, a mother, and a widow, and an old settler of the country; and more especially seeing that the punishment of Forgery is Capital, and therefore in the estimation of the Jury, severe and bordering on vindictive justice.

The *Houston Morning Star* also editorialized that the death penalty for forgery was too severe and implied that Mrs. Mann should receive a lighter sentence. Such pressure as this won executive clemency, then a full pardon for her from President Mirabeau Lamar.

In spite of her many brushes with the law, Mrs. Mann moved in social circles and commanded the respect of many prominent Houston citizens. She could also be civic-minded; when yellow fever and cholera claimed three hundred lives in the first six months of 1838, her hotel was used to house the sick. When her son Flournoy Hunt married Miss Mary Henry in the Mansion House on June 15, 1838, the wedding was the outstanding social event of the season with one attendant calling it a "grand affair." President Houston served as best man with the pretty, designing widow Mrs. Holliday on his arm as maid of honor, while Dr. Ashbel Smith served as second groomsman. This ceremony would seem to indicate that Pamelia and her family were far from ostracized.

The Mansion House entered into a period of decline with the moving of the capital to Waterloo (Austin). As early as September 1837, Congressman Rusk introduced a resolution to appoint a committee to choose a desirable place for relocating the capital. His reason for the resolution was "the disagreeable weather, mud, mud, mud and mostly ... the expected dread yellow fever" of Houston. On October 12, 1839, thirty teams and wagons started the removal of archives and furnishings from the Capitol building to Austin at a cost of $1,100. The empty structure was leased and remodeled as the Capitol Hotel at the corner of Main and Texas streets, the present location of the Rice–Rittenhouse Hotel.[2]

As William Hogan so aptly put it, "Death came at last to this feminine swaggerer along the paths of crime." Pamelia Mann died of natural causes on November 4, 1840, leaving her two sons as the only heirs. Flourney Hunt, the eldest, was appointed administrator of her estate under a bond of $70,000. The court allowed him to sell the household furniture, cattle and hogs to pay his mother's funeral expenses; the total amount rendered by the auctioneers was $2,652.24. The estate assets listed on June 1, 1842, exceeded five thousand dollars in value and included the Mansion House and surrounding lots in Houston, a claim to a quarter section of land, and seven slaves. Reverend O.M. Addison made an astute observation in his "Reminiscences," saying that Pamelia was

> . . .A widow and forced, perhaps from the injustice of others, to step forward in her own defense and meet lawless men on their own grounds; it was but natural that she should have developed the rude and free-spo-

---

2. The Capitol Hotel became widely known as the place where Dr. Anson Jones, the last president of the Republic of Texas, committed suicide. In February 1846, President Jones retired to "Barrington," his cotton and tobacco plantation near Independence, with the ultimate goal of serving in the United States Senate like his predecessor, Sam Houston. An injury ended his practice in 1849 when Dr. Jones was thrown from his horse and left in constant pain with a withered, disabled left arm. The disability made him very moody and inclined to brood over being neglected by the people of Texas. When U.S. Senator Thomas J. Rusk killed himself in 1857 after the death of his wife, Dr. Jones traveled to Austin to personally campaign for the prized vacant seat. However, the final blow to his bruised psyche came in November 1857 when the state legislature chose J. Pinckney Henderson as Rusk's successor with Jones getting not a single vote. The following January the despondent Anson was visiting in Houston when he checked into the Capitol Hotel; upon meeting an old friend in the lobby, he remarked, "My public career began in this house and I have been thinking it might end here." The next morning Jones was found in his room with a bullet through his head.

ken temper of the times and people among whom she lived.

This writer is impressed with the succinct tribute of Mr. Hogan, who said that ". . . one must, in all conscience, remain thankful that the stuffy tediousness of the overpious was relieved by her vagaries."

And what of Pamelia's hotel? In 1846 the Houston post office moved into the old Mansion House. After the building fell in ruins in 1855, a fine, four-story brick hotel called Hutchins House was built on the site in 1859. Thus passed the last reminder of a colorful lady and her era.

IV

GAIL BORDEN: A Texas Success Story

Gail Borden, Jr., is buried at White Plains, New York, and his Borden Company empire began with condensed milk plants in Connecticut and New York, yet he spent much of his adult life and his last winters in Texas. From 1829 until 1851 Texans knew him as a newspaper editor, surveyor, land commissioner, customs collector, civic leader, Baptist pioneer, and inventor. He was helper and adviser to Stephen F. Austin, who trusted him more than any other man. Sam Houston considered his services indispensable during the formative years of the Republic. He was a prime mover behind Galveston's growth into a major city although local residents saw him as the town's leading curiosity and eccentric. His practical inventiveness, varied talents, and devotion to the public good reminded one of a Texas-style Benjamin Franklin.

Young Gail, the first of four sons, was born at Norwich, New York, on November 9, 1801. A year earlier his father, Gail Senior, married Philadelphia Wheeler, a great granddaughter of Roger Williams, who always carried his well-worn family *Bible* with her. In 1800 the Bordens moved from Rhode Island to the New York Chenango Valley, an area controlled by the Oneida Indians only a generation before. When the federal census of

Portrait of Gail Borden, Jr.
Courtesy Public Affairs Department,
Borden, Inc., New York, N.Y.

1810 showed Norwich with a population of 2,700, old Gail felt crowded enough to leave his farm and sawmill and take his family west to Cincinnati. After selling his land for $1,620 in early 1814, he followed the Allegheny to Pittsburgh and bought a Kentucky flatboat, an ark-looking vessel with sideboards and a partial roof. The Borden family then floated down the Ohio River until they reached the Licking River opposite Cincinnati. After the elder Gail surveyed the ferry crossing that became Covington, Kentucky, he moved his family to New London, Indiana, in 1816. It was there that Gail, Jr., attended school for a year and a half in a predominantly Baptist area.

As he grew into manhood, young Gail was elected a militia captain in Jefferson County and made his first land purchase in May 1820. By then he had a thin, stooped appearance and was bothered by a persistent cough. When advised to go to a less rigorous climate for health reasons, Gail and his eighteen-year-old brother Thomas H., decided to strike out for the Southwest. After rafting down river to New Orleans, the two learned that Stephen F. Austin was there staying at the Richardson House. *Empresario* Austin had received a Spanish concession to bring three hundred Louisiana families to Texas and was advertising for recruits in various southern newspapers. Although he met Austin and the two became friends, Gail's frail health was to delay his coming to Texas for almost seven years. He instead accepted the invitation of Dr. William Lattimore to do surveying at his "Green Valley" plantation in southwestern Mississippi. In the early summer of 1822, Gail settled in Amite County but a nagging cough forced him to become a schoolmaster, a position that kept him indoors in bad weather and gave him access to the books in Dr. Lattimore's library. Starting his classes at sunrise, he could be seen running to school carrying a pupil on each shoulder. He was soon teaching two schools and his cough improved enough for Gail to be named Amite County Surveyor in March 1826. When he was twenty-six he married one of his former pupils, sixteen-year-old Penelope Mercer, on March 18, 1828.

In the meantime Thomas Borden had gone to Texas in June 1822 as Austin's official surveyor and one of the "Old Three Hundred" colonists. He and two young companions named Johnson and Walker each received title to one-third of a league of land on the lower Bernard in July 1824. Thomas spent most of his time at the colony headquarters town of San Felipe and he built a home there after marrying Demis Woodward in 1829; the couple had two sons before her death seven years later. Old Gail Borden, a recent widower, also moved to Texas from Indiana with his two youngest sons in 1828 and became a blacksmith at San Felipe.

Young Gail visited Texas in June 1828, saw the opportunities for an ambitious man, and resigned his surveyor job in September 1829. Penelope's father, Eli Mercer, was also bitten by the Texas "bug" and on November 29, 1829, he and his family reached the settlement of Egypt on the Colorado River.[1] Under terms of the state

1. The area known as Egypt originated in a Spanish land grant conveyed by Stephen F. Austin to John C. Clark, one of the "Old Three Hundred" colonists, on July 16, 1824. Clark's league of land ran to the Colorado River and was some ten miles northwest of present Wharton. He brought carefully-wrapped seed corn to Texas and planted fifteen acres in corn by 1827. A severe drought struck the Gulf Coast that year and the only significant rain in present Wharton County fell on Clark's land. As news of his good fortune spread, other colonists came to him for grain and talked of "going down into Egypt for corn" as in the Scriptures. The name stuck and a small settlement called "Egypt" developed near Clark's place at the intersection of the primitive roads connecting Richmond with Texana and Columbus with Matagorda.

In 1836 Eli Mercer started one of the first cotton gins in Texas at Egypt. He also developed a process to make white sugar from the cane growing in the riverbottom fields; Gail Borden praised the quality of this sugar in a *Telegraph* issue of November 1836. Eli was a devout Baptist and true Christian soldier, fighting in the battle of San Jacinto and serving as an original trustee of Baylor University at Independence, chartered by the Republic of Texas in February 1845.

Colonization Law of 1825, both Gail and his father-in-law were entitled to a league (4,428 acres) of Texas land. The Bordens arrived just in time for their first child Mary to be born on Galveston Island on Christmas Eve of 1829. After joining the Mercers at Egypt, Gail lived there for a time and made a half-hearted attempt at farming and stockraising before turning to surveying. On January 30, 1830, *The Texas Gazette* at San Felipe announced that Gail had been named deputy surveyor to serve in brother Tom's absence and he soon moved his family there after buying a town lot for thirty dollars.

Gail first became involved in the Texas revolutionary cause after the Anahuac Insurrection of June 1832. At a "Citizen's Meeting" of the Navidad and Lavaca settlements held at Thomas Menefee's gin, he was named secretary and chosen one of six men to draft protest resolutions which read in part: ". . . It is with deep regret we hear of the necessity of repelling unconstitutional encroachments of any officer of government." After being named to a committee of inquiry and correspondence for the purpose of promoting a convention, Gail represented the Lavaca District at the Convention of April, 1833,

---

Mercer died at Egypt on December 7, 1872.

In 1832 John Clark sold one-half of his Egypt grant, some two thousand acres, to Captain William Jones Elliot Heard, another San Jacinto veteran. The Heard family had come to Texas from Tennessee as part of Austin's second colony and settled near Texana in December 1830. Relying solely on childhood memories of fine homes, Captain Heard in 1847 started construction of a double dog-run house on the highest point of his prairie land. He built it as he went with no plans and the classic pink-brick Georgian home was completed in 1849. Slaves made the bricks from the banks of Caney Creek, the interior pine wood was hauled by oxcart from East Texas, and there were twin chimneys in the gabled ends. Captain Heard eventually moved to Chappell Hill and died there while his Egypt plantation was inherited by his daughter and son-in-law, Elizabeth and Mentor Northington. Today the sixth generation of the Heard–Northington family still lives on Egypt plantation, one thousand acres of working farmland. In 1975 George Northington III, and his wife Anita added a new bedroom, kitchen, and keeping room (family living room) to the back of the original home. "Egypt" is one of a half dozen of Texas's original plantations that is still owned by the same family that started it.

45

Gail Borden and his wife, Emeline Eunice Eno Church Borden, vacationing at Niagara Falls.

Courtesy Public Affairs Department,
Borden, Inc., New York, N.Y.

John Gail Borden, his father's favorite child, succeeded as second president of the New York Condensed Milk Company.

Courtesy Public Affairs Department,
Borden, Inc., New York, N.Y.

Henry Lee Borden, eldest son of Gail Borden and third president of the New York Condensed Milk Company.

Courtesy Public Affairs Department,
Borden, Inc., New York, N.Y.

which drafted a proposed state constitution and sent Stephen Austin to Mexico City with a series of demands including separate statehood within the Mexican federal system. Before leaving, Austin admonished Gail, "For God's sake, do not let my people do anything foolish or rash while I am away." During his eighteen-month absence and subsequent imprisonment in Mexico City, Gail was left in charge of the land office under the direction of Samuel M. Williams, the colonial secretary. Williams, however, was deeply involved in both land speculation and military intrigues with Governor Augustin Viesca and spent much of his time in Saltillo and Monclova in 1834 and 1835. Gail was thus left alone at San Felipe to face a barrage of requests and disputes over land matters.

The Bordens suffered a personal tragedy in August 1833 when daughter Mary died. On January 29, 1835, Gail wrote to W.C. White and James F. Perry at Columbia to seek their help in starting a newspaper at San Felipe, which had a weekly paper for four years until the press was leased to Brazoria for printing the *Texas Republican* there. During this same period brother Thomas went to New Orleans and purchased a Smith medium hand press. In June 1835 Gail received a request from Henry McDowell, the owner of a New Orleans engraving shop, who asked him to compile a pocket map of Texas. Although no proof exists that Borden honored the request, the letter does suggest that he may have prepared the first topographical map of Texas. In early September Gail and his brother John P. went to visit Austin, who had just been released from prison and was resting at his sister's home, Peach Point, below Brazoria. After some long conversations together, the two brothers accompanied Austin to the dinner held in his honor at Jane Long's hotel on September 8. When the "Father of Texas" left San Felipe on October 8 to take command of the volunteer Texas army gathered at Gonzales, he appointed a committee of five from different municipalities to serve as a governmental authority until the Consultation met; Gail was chosen to represent San Felipe on the committee.

By October 1835 Texas was at war with Mexico. Gail was now to serve his adopted land with pen rather than sword as the Thomas Paine of the Texas Revolution. On October 10 the press of "Baker and Bordens" produced the first edition of *The Telegraph and Texas Register* at San Felipe with Gail and Thomas Borden and translator Joseph Baker announcing their intent to be ". . . a faithful register of passing events." The paper contained eight pages and was to be published every Saturday at a subscription rate of five dollars a year. From the very beginning, Gail gave himself completely to the paper, the official organ of the de facto government and the only source of battlefield news during the revolution. The October 17 edition included an editorial titled "Texas Patriotism." He refused to stoop to character assassination and avoided taking sides or giving political advice. Borden did, however, feel duty-bound to provide moral instruction and once reached the rather startling conclusion that drunkenness might lead to "spontaneous combustion of the human body." During the war he faced many personnel and logistical problems: His brother Tom and Baker left the paper to join the army; editions had to be skipped due to lack of paper; customers on the move made it difficult to deliver papers and collect subscriptions. But Gail persevered; in a letter to Colonel Austin, he stated, "My maxim is: Do the best for my country, praise or no praise."

While the Consultation was meeting at San Felipe to organize a provisional state government, Borden heard a Sam Houston oration as to why Texas must be prepared to take up arms. After talking with the general, he wrote to Austin on November 5, 1835, and remarked, ". . . I believe he has the interest of our country at heart. He made the best speech yesterday I ever heard . . ." Gail took on added responsibilities on October 21, 1835, when he was appointed collector to receive all land dues for the Department of Brazos. As the war progressed he proposed that all Texas landowners "hypothecate" one-half of their holdings to boost Texas credit, pledging one league himself. When Austin was named as one of three commissioners to the United States, he carried in his suitcases one million dollars worth of Texas bonds printed by Borden in the *Telegraph* office.

The March 5, 1836, issue of the *Telegraph* included a historic statement at the bottom of the last page: news from Washington-on-the-Brazos only twenty miles away was received just in time to print a brief excerpt below the headline, "Texas Has Declared Her Independence." When Gail later printed a handbill containing the full text of the Declaration of Independence and its signers, he omitted the names of its authors, George Childress and Sterling C. Robertson. The news of the fall of the Alamo reached San Felipe a few nights after the March 12 issue, prompting men to pack their possessions, take their families and flee. But Borden stayed at his post, saying simply, "My presence is so essential here."

Among the units in Sam Houston's retreating Texas army was a company of forty men raised by Captain Mosely Baker at San Felipe, including the two youngest Borden brothers, John P. and Paschal. When the army reached San Felipe on March 27, General Houston chose to march up the Brazos to Groce's Landing. This decision was challenged by Captain Baker, who wanted to stand and fight at San Felipe; in fact, his company defiantly stayed behind to defend the river crossing. After Baker finally ordered the town to be burned, the *Telegraph* building was the first to be put to the torch but Gail got his printing press across the river by ferryboat on March 30. At this time the Bordens were invited to relocate their paper at Harrisburg and serve as the official press of the ad interim government headed by President David

G. Burnet. Gail then wrote Burnet asking the government to send a large wagon and team to remove the press to Harrisburg but received no response. He then camped a week on the flooded prairie while John P. hurried to Egypt for Eli Mercer's wagon and team. The heavy wagon could make only ten miles a day with Gail and Joseph Baker walking alongside all the way to Harrisburg, arriving there on April 12. While Baker left to join Houston's army at San Jacinto, Borden found a vacant house to work in and had issue number twenty-two set for printing on April 14. After apologizing that there had been no paper since March 24, Gail made the following defiant statement:

> We promise the public of our beloved country that our press will never cease its operation until our silence shall announce to them that there is no more in Texas a resting place for a free press nor for a government of the people.

Before the paper could be struck off, elements of the Mexican army arrived. Gail and President Burnet's Cabinet had only an hour to escape when they boarded a steamboat bound for Galveston at noon on April 15. There was no time to move the printing press so three heroic and unknown printers stayed behind in the deserted Harrisburg and ran off six copies of the paper before General Santa Anna arrived that evening. He burned the town, dumped the press into the murky waters of Bray's Bayou, and proceeded to his own date with destiny at San Jacinto.

At Galveston Gail was reunited with brother Thomas, who had taken their families and father there. Thomas's home and cotton gin at Fort Bend had been destroyed by Santa Anna when he crossed the Brazos there by ferry. The Bordens found themselves among some one thousand refugees camping in the open on Galveston Island. After receiving news of the Battle of San Jacinto, the Borden brothers obtained a small boat in early May

1836 and landed at Fort Bend where they found all of Thomas's property burned and ransacked. They held a family conference on the spot and decided that Gail and John P. would resume their surveying work and be land agents while Thomas was to plant a corn crop.

Within a few weeks Gail and Thomas were in New Orleans hoping to buy another press on credit; failing that, they returned to Velasco where they presented the interim government with a bill for $982.50 to cover the five weeks of public printing done by the *Telegraph* prior to March 25. Their work included such revered documents as the Declaration of Independence, Travis's letter from Bexar, and news of the fall of the Alamo. However, the Burnet government had no funds so their bill went unpaid. Only by traveling to Cincinnati and mortgaging their Texas lands was Thomas able to buy a printing press in June 1836. In July the brothers relocated at Columbia, the first capital of the Republic of Texas, where their first *Telegraph* issue appeared on August 2 with the motto, "We go for our country." The newspaper became a semi-weekly with minimum operating expenses of $144 a week. In the first Columbia issue, the constitution of the Republic was published for the first time in Texas. It seems that the secretary of the convention at Washington-on-the-Brazos had taken the original draft to the United States where it was lost. However, a copy of the document was first published in Nashville in June, then in Cincinnati in July. While Thomas Borden was in that Ohio city buying a press, he obtained a copy of the constitution and printed it at Columbia as the official version. When Tom's wife died of fever on September 15, 1836, he seemed to lose his taste for the newspaper business. By then Gail was worn out and in poor health so the brothers in late October announced their intention to sell out.

Gail strongly supported his old friend, Stephen F. Austin, in the Texas presidential election held in September 1836. On August 15 he wrote to advise Austin that he could not be elected unless the people were convinced that he was not implicated in the past land frauds and speculations involving Samuel Williams. Borden even went so far as to say, "I have offered . . . to give my life on the question . . . if at any time it should be found that you were engaged in the affair." He suggested a "circular to the people" and Austin complied in an open letter to Gail printed as a handbill. Ironically, that same issue of the *Telegraph* which carried Austin's letter also announced Sam Houston's belated entry into the campaign. Seemingly indifferent to the outcome, Austin was beaten badly by the general in the election.

The day after the First Texas Congress convened on October 3, 1836, Gail's *Telegraph* spelled out the needs of the Republic in a lengthy article titled "A Few Ideas for Consideration." He saw his role as that of an advocate of public policy and the session evidently pleased him; when Congress adjourned in December, Gail was moved to write his appreciation. During these months he was a constant companion of the sick Austin and was standing by sobbing when his old friend died of pneumonia at Judge McKinstry's Columbia home on December 27, 1836; the next *Telegraph* issue ran the poignant headline, "The Patriarch Has Left Us." Two months before his death, Austin had written brother-in-law James F. Perry telling of his desire to visit the United States and admitting that Gail was the only person he could trust to close the land business. After his demise the archives of Austin's four colonies were taken to Peach Point where Gail and John P. classified and indexed them and compiled a map of his colonial grants, a monumental task which took several months. The brothers received $2500 for their efforts and President Houston in 1837 named John Borden as the first commissioner of the General Land Office. When Mr. Perry organized a statewide committee in 1844 to collect documents on Austin's life, Gail was one of those authorized to receive the materials.

Throughout the autumn of 1836 the firm of Borden and Company also did surveying work. That September Gail and his friend, Moses Lapham, began to lay off town lots for the new city of Houston, completing the task in late November. During the project Moses came down with chills and fever and resorted to huge draughts of black pepper as a medicinal remedy. The illness prompted a letter to his father in Ohio in which Lapham mentioned how unhealthy the site was. The town was surveyed on a northeast-southwest axis so as to maximize the effect of the prevailing southeastern Gulf breeze. They located all of Houston to the south of Buffalo Bayou and its seventeen streets and five public squares followed the twisting of that stream.

After Tom Borden sold his interest in the paper to Dr. Francis Moore, Jr., on March 9, 1837, the *Telegraph* relocated at Houston on April 16. Gail and Dr. Moore had been promised a "nearly completed" building; finding none, they were forced to rent a shanty but the first Houston issue came out on May 2. The paper soon took on a vitriolic tone with Dr. Moore's editorial column lambasting the followers of Sam Houston. Gail, the ever-more-uncomfortable senior partner, found buyer Jacob W. Cruger for his share of the paper and completed the transfer on June 20, 1837. Borden had guided the *Telegraph* through twenty tumultuous months but once he sold out, he broke completely with his newspaper past.

In the early summer of 1837, Gail became a public servant when President Houston appointed him as the Republic's first collector of customs at Galveston. The site was a natural collecting station but not much of a town; at that time the residents were sleeping in hammocks to avoid the snakes. Borden's first Galveston home for his wife and four small children was built in half a day! This "box house" was a ten by eleven foot room made of sod-grass while Gail's first office was Juan Bradburn's old Mexican cypress customhouse. At first he had trouble with smugglers operating on Bolivar Peninsula since that area was outside his jurisdiction; nevertheless, he collected a total of $25,530.77 during his first three months on the job. On October 4, 1837, a new two-story customhouse was completed on the northwest corner of Strand and Tremont streets; two days later a great storm wrecked and blew it out to sea. During the next year the collector had to use a rented brig, the *Perserverance*, as his headquarters. The storm tides did teach Galveston residents a lesson: the next customhouse and other buildings were raised four feet off the ground.

During the fourteen years that Galveston was Gail's home, he left his mark on the city. There was no local civil government on the island during the fall and winter of 1837 so he played sheriff, once going so far as to attempt to arrest a man for stealing. Port business increased steadily; in February 1838 five ships entered the harbor in one hour. President Houston visited that May and said he was highly pleased with Gail's operation. The next month Borden drew up definite written operating rules for the customhouse. The Republic's income for 1838 was $367,000 with $235,000 of that coming from customs and one-half of those receipts collected at Galveston. However, politics cut Borden's tenure short after a town meeting in the spring of 1838 resulted in a group of citizens endorsing Mirabeau B. Lamar for president of Texas. On June 9 the *Telegraph* carried a protest signed by Gail and ten others announcing their support for Peter Grayson, who was later to commit suicide. After being elected to the office on December 10, 1838, Lamar fired Borden three days later, replacing him with Dr. Willis Roberts.

The jobless Gail then joined forces with Michel Menard, a member of the Galveston City Company. Born to French parents in 1805 at Montreal, Canada, Menard worked with fur trappers as an Indian trader and first appeared in Texas in November 1829. He represented

Liberty at the Convention of 1836, signed the Texas Declaration of Independence, and on December 9, 1836, paid the Republic $50,000 to quitclaim the one league and one labor earlier granted him on Galveston Island by the Mexican government. Known as the promoter of "that wild project of Galveston," Menard organized the Galveston City Company on April 13, 1838, and was elected as its first president. The company proceeded to lay off all the streets, then to advertise and sell all the town lots. In May 1839 Borden was named agent of the company, then secretary in 1842, and helped sell 2,500 city lots before resigning in 1851. He owned eight island lots by 1840, and the federal census of 1850 showed him as the owner of Galveston real estate valued at $100,000. When the first city elections were held on March 14, 1839, Gail was elected an alderman and immediately took the lead in raising the moral tone of the island. His first concern was the host of gamblers who had flocked there and camped out in tents. Borden introduced an ordinance to suppress gambling and twenty men were appointed as special constables to enforce it while the city council went so far as to issue a proclamation giving gamblers only hours to leave the city. Gail also had time to push through regulations for saloons before resigning for health reasons on June 18, 1839.

When the *Neptune* docked at Galveston on January 24, 1840, one of those on board was the Reverend James Huckins, who was sent to Texas as Missionary Agent of the American Baptist Home Mission Society. He was bound for Houston but was persuaded to stay a day and preach in town. Encouraged by the several hundred who attended his three services, Huckins agreed to stay and organize a church. On January 30, 1840, a meeting was held in the home of Thomas Borden where the First Baptist Church of Galveston was organized with nine charter members. That night, Gail, Penelope and her sister stepped forward at the Invitation time and asked to be baptized. Reverend Huckins conducted their baptismal service in the Gulf of Mexico and a crowd of fifty saw the three embrace and weep as they waded back to the beach. In October 1841 Borden attended the second meeting of the Union Baptist Association held at Clear Creek in Fayette County. There he was named a trustee of the Texas Baptist Education Society, the founder of Baylor University. He was later to serve as clerk, deacon, choir leader, and Sunday School superintendent of the Galveston First Baptist Church; in fact, his "glorious" and "best" plan ever was a scheme to convert all Roman Catholics by giving the children attractive Protestant tracts. However, a stormy period in his religious life came in 1848 when Gail became angry with the visiting revivalist, Rufus C. Burleson. The more liberal Borden objected to Burleson's emphasis on the doctrine of baptism and asked that the meeting be opened to Methodist and Presbyterian ministers. Burleson stood his ground and the argument ended when three Borden children made Professions of Faith and were baptized during the revival, inspiring Gail to tell Rufus to preach as he pleased.

Sam Houston's election as president of Texas in 1841 led to Borden's reappointment to the Galveston collectorship on December 24, 1841. After General Adrian Woll and a Mexican army of 1400 captured and held San Antonio for nine days in September 1842, Houston placed Gail in charge of repelling a possible sea attack on Galveston. The collector became the focal point of controversy after the Texas Congress in July 1842 passed legislation requiring that all duties paid in Texas paper money ("Exchequer Bills") must be received at their market value, about thirty cents on the dollar at the time. Gail disagreed with this policy and decided to raise its value by crediting the paper money at eighty cents, a loss of fifty cents on the dollar for the Texas government. When the Treasury Department objected and speculators began to deal in the bills, Borden offered his resignation on September 22, 1842, but President Houston refused to accept it and replied:

> This I know; you have as much interest in the country as I have, and if you think the country can dispense with your services, every useful officer may think so too . . . What will be the consequences? Anarchy!!! . . .

Gail held stubbornly to his policy and felt vindicated when exchequer bills rose to seventy cents on the dollar by the spring of 1843. He resigned again that April; this time Houston accepted and wrote him a brusque, scolding letter. Borden then refused to turn over $27,000 in customhouse funds in his possession so as to protect himself against possible suits. This controversy was not settled until 1848 with Gail all the while serene in the belief that he had done what was right.

The Borden's fourth son, John Gail, was born on January 4, 1844, but tragedy struck the following August when Penelope was exposed to yellow fever while walking along the Galveston docks. She was only thirty-two when she died on September 5, leaving Gail alone to raise five children. On February 15, 1845, he married the widow Mrs. Augusta Stearns, a woman his own age. From the beginning it was a marriage of convenience with both going their separate ways. They delighted in needling each other; Gail made it a point to introduce her as his second wife while Augusta loved to make fun of her husband at mealtime. By 1848 Borden was paying taxes on five slaves, 350 head of cattle, eight city lots, and 13,700 other Texas acres. Following the lead of his father, Old Gail at Richmond, he helped to organize a local temperance society in May 1848.

A tinkerer at heart, Gail worked on many ideas and inventions in the 1840s. His natural curiosity led him to follow the advice he once gave a friend: "As fast as you drop one thing, seize upon another." His Galveston projects included a portable bathhouse for both sexes, an ether-filled refrigerator to house people and thus freeze yellow fever out of existence, cans of condensed chicken, turkey, and beef as well as such food extracts as bread made from finely ground bones and jelly from oxen horns and hoofs. Gail even invited a select group of friends to take a moonlight demonstration ride on his "terraqueous machine," a prairie schooner mounting mast and sails that would operate on both land and sea. After a team of horses pulled this combination wagon-sailboat to the beach and the passengers boarded, the trade winds ripped into the billowing sails and propelled the strange vehicle to a speed of ten miles per hour; at that point some of the faint-hearted ladies began to scream and implore Borden to stop. When the vessel was suddenly turned into the surf, it capsized and all aboard received a good Gulf bath!

Gail's greatest idea, the meat biscuit, was inspired by "pinole," the main Comanche food made of dried buffalo meat, hominy and mesquite beans. He first became sensitive to the food-supply problems for travelers, soldiers and sailors after hearing of the "Forty-Niners" and the gold rush to California. Borden started experimenting with dehydrated meat compounded with flour in mid-1849, obtained his American patent on February 5, 1850, and was listed as a manufacturer of meat biscuit in the federal census of that year. His boiling process reduced eleven pounds of meat to one pound of extract which was then mixed with flour at a ratio of two pounds of extract glue to three pounds of flour. Baking reduced this five pounds of meat dough to four pounds of meat biscuit which looked like a hard well-dried meat loaf that could either be fried or baked. Needing an urbane, polished agent to market his product, Gail turned to Dr. Ashbel Smith, who was then living a life of idle ease at Evergreen plantation in Brazoria County.

In May 1850 the United States Army first tested the meat biscuit at Fort Leavenworth, Kansas, where it was

given an enthusiastic endorsement by Brevet Colonel
E. V. Sumner of the First Dragoons, who wrote Gail and
said:

> I have tried the meat biscuit and find it all and
> more than the inventor thinks it is. To satisfy myself I
> have lived upon it entirely for several successive days
> and I am content that I could live upon it for months
> and retain my health and strength. In my judgment it
> is a very great discovery and must lead to important
> results. I am decidedly of the opinion that we ought to
> commence using it in the army at once and I believe
> from all active operations in the field the advantages of
> this food will be so apparent that it will become in gen-
> eral use in a few years.

A similar response also came from General Thomas Lawson, Surgeon-General of the United States Army. After
Secretary of War Charles Conrad ordered enough meat
biscuit that October to "give the article a fair trial," Gail
spent $10,000, mortgaged his land for financing, and
built a two-story brick factory with a ten-horsepower engine. This plant at the corner of Strand and Rosenberg
streets in Galveston had the capacity to boil 7,000 pounds
of beef a day.

During those giddy early days of all-out meat biscuit
production, an Austin newspaper asserted that "a man
can now mount his horse with a month's rations in his
saddle pockets and he needs no other cooking utensil
than a tin cup." A circular of the period made the following incredible claims for this miracle product: The meat
biscuit makes the finest known soup; it reaches its highest perfection when boiled with vegetables; it is irresisti-
ble in a pot pie; it gives a superb pudding when mixed
with rice and sugar; it is a perfect background for a mince
pie and may be used as a custard by merely varying the
flavoring.

It was Dr. Smith's idea to take the meat biscuit to
the London World's Fair of 1851 and the Great Council
Exhibition held there that May. On March 7, 1851, Gov-

ernor Peter H. Bell appointed Smith as the Texas delegate to the fair. After resigning his position with the Galveston City Company, Borden left a month later bound for London; he simply could not pass up the opportunity to show his product to such potential customers as the emperor of Russia and the British Navy. The United States was allowed 80,000 square feet of display space in the Crystal Palace but there were only a handful of American exhibits including artificial teeth, Samuel Colt's revolver, Cyrus McCormick's "Virginia Reaper," and two barrels of Borden meat biscuit. As a result of the showing, the jury awarded Gail the highest award possible, the Great Council Gold Medal, for his contribution to the foodstuffs industry. He also received an English patent that September and was elected an honorary member of the London Society of Arts in 1852. While the two Texas partners were still in England, they met in a London hotel in July 1851 to divide the world for marketing purposes: Gail was to handle the United States while Dr. Smith would embark on a world-wide selling tour.

In the midst of all this acclaim and optimistic planning, the United States Army issued the damaging "Waco Report" on June 21, 1851, after an extended biscuit trial. Six army officers concluded that the meat biscuit produced headache and nausea, lowered resistance to heat and cold, had a disgusting flavor, and did not satisfy hunger; in short, it was not a substitute for ordinary army rations and the officers unanimously recommended against its adoption. Upon his return to the United States, the stung Borden traveled to Washington, D.C., the headquarters of army and navy contractors in beeves, beans and bread. He quickly discovered that these long-time contractors had considerable influence with key politicians with whom they shared profits. After facing long delays and being shuttled from one office to another, the stymied Gail sought out his old friend, Senator Sam Houston, who admitted being forced to play the "same game" forty years earlier while representing the Arkansas Cherokees in the capital. Old Sam told Borden that his reward for accusing some contractors of gouging the Indians was to be denounced as an imposter and fraud; although he had the satisfaction of caning one such critic, a Ohio Congressman, to "within an inch of his life," the frustrated Houston finally gave up and returned to Arkansas.

Borden labeled the Waco Report a villainous plot linked to outside pressure from meat packers and producers while Horace Greeley of the *New York Tribune* declared that the "government had treated him most rascally." Nevertheless, the damage had been done; by the winter of 1851 his Galveston plant had 34,000 pounds of meat biscuit in stock while a combination of heavy expenses and few sales forced Gail to admit, "I am entirely out of money . . ." By this time he had moved to New York City to seek out customers in hospital kitchens and ship galleys, only to encounter young doctors who laughed at him and ship cooks who would not take the time to prepare the meat biscuit properly. Borden met with total indifference in 1852 when he contacted all departing New York ships and finally ended his biscuit efforts in 1853 after spending $60,000 and going deeply in debt. For more than four years, he kept writing troubled, doleful letters to his inactive partner at Evergreen, Dr. Smith. December 1854 found Gail back at Galveston to "look over the wreck of his fortunes."

A decade earlier Borden had predicted to young Parson Baker that he would eventually condense milk so as to make it lasting and dependable. Using only the pots, pans and vats in his crude Galveston lab behind the fig orchard, he had discovered that milk evaporated in vacuo could be condensed without impurities, a notable breakthrough indeed since bacteria, germs and microbes would not be discovered and named for another twenty years. Tradition has it that Gail was moved to pursue this new idea of condensed milk while sailing home from London in the fall of 1851. When the cows on board either died or the rough seas made them too seasick to be milked, the crying of ill and hungry babies so distressed Borden that he vowed to find a pure milk product. His basic idea was to preserve milk, retaining the fat but removing the water by evaporation in a vacuum pan to prevent contamination. This unique treatment of milk would maintain its purity and freshness for weeks while retaining its natural qualities.

While living a hand-to-mouth existence in 1853 at a little Shaker village near New Lebanon, New York, Gail's experiments led him to conclude that *any* exposure during the evaporation process would spoil the product; *only* milk evaporated in a vacuum pan was dependable. He was unaware of past and similar scientific efforts in both France and England when he ordered a vacuum pan in February 1853, then applied for both American and English patents for condensing milk in a vacuum on May 1 of that year. In December 1853 Gail wrote Dr. Smith and remarked, ". . . I have invented a new process for the concentration and preservation of milk . . ." From this time forward condensed milk was to be his consuming passion.

His first patent application was rejected because it lacked "novelty and usefulness." The Patent Office defended its decision by replying, "You allege great importance to working entirely in vacuum. This office does not have faith in such an allegation." They did not consider the exclusion of air during evaporation to be a unique feature of the discovery; changing their minds would take Gail three years and three rejections. During this interval he obtained evidence and affidavits from Robert Macfarlane, editor of *Scientific American*, and John Currie, head of the prestigous Belmont laboratories, to the effect that his method was unequaled by evaporation in open air or any other process. By September 1855 Borden was flat broke when he wrote his last long letter to Dr. Smith. It reveals both his religious faith and innate optimism and reads in part:

> ... You ask how Uncle Gail holds on. Well the answer is simple. The religion of Jesus Christ as set forth in the Gospel sustains me as it will anyone who puts his trust in it. I have my little son John, a pious child, and we read God's Holy word together and pray together. In this way I am sustained, my friend ... I am happy to inform you that I have succeeded in concentrating milk 80% without the use of sugar and it is soluble in either hot or cold water. It is a beautiful article. I do not hesitate to tell you that should I live two years I shall present the world an invention of vast importance. Milk will be as common on shipboard as sugar. Remember what Uncle Gail has told you. He will be the inventor of this great process.

Finally, on August 19, 1856, Borden was awarded an American patent for condensing milk in a vacuum over low heat. His one original scientific contribution was the discovery that air must be excluded in the evaporation process. He was the first to realize that milk, like blood, is a living fluid that begins to die and decompose as soon as it is drawn from the cow.

Gail's family life suffered during the three-year patent fight, a time when he and son John were living on one dollar a day. He separated from his wife Augusta and nothing more is known of her although he did remarry in 1860. Meanwhile, back in Texas, his oldest daughter Philadelphia married widower Captain A. Swift on February 7, 1855. Swift was thirty years old and the father of four. The seventeen-year-old bride waited a month to even tell her father, then was left alone to raise the newfound family when her husband died on April 13, 1855. She later married J.W. Johnson and they settled at Columbus in the early 1870s.

In the summer of 1856, Darius Miner, a store owner from Wolcottville, Connecticut, found Gail an old abandoned carriage plant for his first factory but it failed when he was unable to find buyers for condensed milk. After returning to Galveston to sell land for capital, Borden tried again in May 1857, serving as his own chief mechanic to fix up an abandoned mill building at Burrville, Connecticut. However, operations also ceased there after the Panic of 1857 dried up his source of financing. His business future was looking bleak indeed until Gail took a fateful train ride to New York City in February 1858. By pure chance he happened to sit next to Jeremiah Milbank, a New York wholesale grocer. The earnest, sincere inventor must have done a good selling job: in an hour Milbank agreed to be his partner and furnish the capital needed for a long shot investment. Borden then returned to Burrville to complete the plant and founded the New York Condensed Milk Company with himself as president.

From the beginning he contracted to take all the output of area dairy farmers at his receiving dock but insisted on sanitary conditions and dirt-free milk. The walls and floors of his factory were white-washed and all workers were dressed in white. Gail would not accept milk that was over fifty-eight degrees fahrenheit and also refused to take milk on Sunday. Four quarts of fresh milk were condensed to one quart, placed in ice-covered sealed cans for shipment, then sold for twenty-five cents a quart. In building his New York market, Borden carried samples from house to house in a handbag, then served his product from a pushcart. His standards of cleanliness attracted a powerful ally in New Yorker Frank Leslie, who in 1858 conducted a crusade against infant mortality and "milk murder" in *Leslie's Illustrated Newspaper*. After carrying a series of articles spotlighting the filth and disease prevalent in New York's milk "distilleries," Leslie was pleased to run Gail's first advertisement for condensed milk on May 22, 1858; it read as follows:

Borden's Condensed Milk prepared in Litchfield County, Connecticut, is the only milk ever concentrated without the admixture of sugar or some other substance and remaining soluble in water. It is simply fresh country milk from which the water has been evaporated.

Within two years the New York Condensed Milk Company prospered to the point that Gail needed a better plant location in more dense dairy country. A horse and buggy search led him to the village of Wassaic, New York, eighty-five miles above New York City. This new factory site was near the Harlem Railway and surrounded by dairy pastures. Gail also witnessed to his Wassaic workers when he had the opportunity, wanting them to know Jesus Christ as he did; to that end he preached a revival at nearby Amenia and taught a young people's Sunday School class. He also married again during this period, taking Mrs. Emeline Eunice Church as his bride on August 15, 1860.

The outbreak of the Civil War spurred the completion of the Wassaic plant in June 1861. Borden's partner, Jeremiah Milbank, decided to provide all-out financial support with the goal of supplying Union troops with condensed milk. The first government order came on June 28, 1862, and Gail sold 50,000 quarts within three months. As his milk came into use in hospitals and camps and became a regular Union field ration, Borden was pressed to keep up with demand. By June 1863 the Wassaic plant was producing 14,000 quarts of milk daily with an assured market for every ounce. In 1864 he built his "perfect" plant, one with a daily capacity of 20,000 quarts, at Brewster, New York, fifty-five miles from New York City. Gail also moved to Brewster and built a two-and one-half-story white colonial mansion there. While commuting to the city, he developed the habit of passing out nickels and dimes to little boys and tramps as he walked to the train station and arranged to have *Bibles* placed in each Harlem Railway coach. In 1865 another condensed milk plant was built at Elgin, Illinois, while a new product name, "Eagle Brand," was adopted in January 1866.

Although Gail was the most celebrated living Texan and had spent most of his adult life there, his first loyalty was to the federal Union; it was simply a matter of loving his whole country more than he loved Texas. However, the Borden family circle was broken by the war years. Gail's son, Henry Lee, served with the Thirty-Fifth Texas Cavalry but young John Gail was a New York Union soldier. Gail's brothers, Thomas H. and John P., had three sons who fought in the Confederate army. In 1863 old Gail Borden died at age eighty-six at Galveston and his youngest son Paschal passed away at Fort Bend the next year.

Although the Civil War assured his fortune, all of Gail's war efforts were not directed toward profit; in fact, his concern about the problem of troop dysentery prompted a very generous offer. During the conflict he told the people living around his Winsted, Connecticut, branch factory that if they would gather and bring in blackberries, he would condense the juice to jelly at no cost to the government. Large quantities of this jelly, a remedy for scourge, were then shipped to General Sherman's troops to counter an epidemic.

The end of the war found Borden convinced that death was near, anxious to see his grandchildren, and homesick for Texas. His first vacation ever was a triumphant homecoming trip in late 1867. By then the Borden Manufacturing Company included a sawmill at Bastrop and Gail was eyeing still another business venture, a beef canning plant. At this time the Southern Pacific Railroad terminated at Columbus but the company was starting to build to the west. The army of construction workers seemed to provide a market for canned roast beef so Gail in 1872 built a canning plant twelve miles west of Columbus at a place he called Borden. His oldest son,

66

Henry Lee, took charge of this new enterprise, the Borden Meat Preserving Company.[2] Gail also built homes for himself and his son on the hills of nearby Harvey's Creek and brother John located there too. Since daughter Philadelphia and his grandchildren were living at nearby Columbus, Gail began to spend four to five months each winter at his modest home at Borden, Texas.

His last trips to Texas came in the spring and fall of 1873. He and brothers Tom and John attended the Texas Veterans Association meeting in Houston that year. Philanthropy took much of his time as he helped to build Texas schools and churches and gave financial support to ministers, teachers and students. In the autumn of 1873, Gail, his wife, and grandson Gail Borden Johnson spent a month visiting with Tom at his Galveston home. While there the stooped and visibly-aging inventor celebrated his seventy-second birthday with Dr. Ashbel Smith as special guest at the party. After going on to his Harvey's Creek home, Gail developed pneumonia shortly after Christmas and died at Borden on Sunday, January 11, 1874. He was buried in the Woodlawn Cemetery at White Plains, New York, where a huge granite milk can marking the burial site was removed to receive his body. The words on Gail's grave monument read simply:

I tried and failed,
I tried again and again, and succeeded.

Texans would say "Amen" to that.

2. The Borden beef canning plant was abandoned soon after Gail's death, leaving a warehouse full of unsold canned meat. After the plant was demolished in 1885, the State of Texas in 1936 erected an historical marker on the site, which was also near Gail's home. Today this marker can be easily spotted on a gently rolling pasture near the banks of Harvey's Creek.

V

The Saga of
Cynthia Ann and Quanah Parker

One of the most enduring frontier tales in Texas history concerns a white woman and her half-breed Indian son. Cynthia Ann Parker was taken captive by Indians as a young girl; a quarter century later she was rescued from her Indian family and tragically returned to civilization and a premature death. The Indian boy who lost his mother was destined to be the famous last chief of the Comanches, a leader who was feared, hated, honored and claimed by Texas. Although they were forcibly separated for life, the bonds of love and devotion between mother and son were never broken. This is their story, the saga of Cynthia Ann and Quanah Parker.

It was pioneer wanderlust that carried John and Sally White Parker and their six sons from Virginia to Georgia, then Tennessee, and finally to Crawford County, Illinois, in 1814. All of the Parkers were hard-working farmers and devout "Hardshell" Baptists, men of the Bible who believed in Closed Communion and held to a stern, Puritanical code of morality. One of the sons, Silas, married Lucy Duty in 1827. Their legendary daughter Cynthia Ann was born that year followed by son John in 1830.

Daniel Parker, the eldest son, decided to move to Mexican Texas in 1830, find land for the clan to settle, and organize a Baptist church. Upon his arrival in February 1831, he was informed that Mexican law forbade such a church. Undeterred, Daniel returned to Illinois, organized a congregation there, and brought its thirty-six members, including the entire Parker family, to Texas in 1832. After the Parkers lived for some eighteen months in present Grimes County, Daniel in 1833 started the first non-Catholic church in Texas, the Pilgrim Predestination Regular Baptist Church, at Elkhart in Anderson County and served as pastor there until his death in December 1844.

In the spring of 1834, Silas and James Parker started building Fort Parker, a log stockade located two miles from present Groesbeck and near the headwaters of the Navasota River. The fort consisted of one acre of wooden stockade walls which enclosed seven split-log cabins and two block houses built at diagonal corners. The fifteen-foot-high cedar walls had pointed logs on top, portholes, and the upper story of the blockhouses jutted over the lower with openings in the floor allowing perpendicular shooting from above. This configuration allowed firing vantage points to rake every side and angle of the fort. There was a clearing around the stockade, a fine spring of water nearby, and farm fields with rich soil some distance away and out of sight. The patriarch of the settlement was Elder John Parker, then seventy-six years old, while eight families of thirty-four hardy pioneers lived in and around the fort. The Parkers had pushed further onto the Brazos bottoms than any whites had gone and knew they were crowding the Comanche range to the northwest. Thus their routine included such precautions as spending nights within the compound walls and traveling in a body when they went to work their fields a mile distant on the Navasota River.

The Comanches, a Ute Indian word meaning

"enemy," were indeed a cause for concern. From the 1650s on they had engaged in an ultimately successful war of extermination with the Lipan Apaches for the buffalo plains of West Texas. At the peak of their power in the early 1800s, they numbered some 20,000 in five main bands and occupied the Llano Estacado (Staked Plain) extending to the vicinity of Austin and San Antonio. From 1820 until 1875 they were the most feared of all Texas enemies. Comanches were the greatest horse-warriors in the West, always fought on horseback, and would travel hundreds of miles in lightning hit-and-run raids for horses. Each male was a warrior and was likely to own 250 horses. They wore buffalo horn headdresses, painted their bodies red, and were fierce, cruel fighters. These Indians lived a nomadic life, never planted seeds of any type, and camped in buffalo-hide teepees located near running water. They stayed only a few days at one campsite and moved quickly in case of an epidemic. The buffalo was the lifeblood of their culture and provided food, clothing, shelter, weapons, tools and utensils.

For a time, however, Texas revolutionary politics caused the Parkers to forget the Comanche threat. Silas and James represented the Viesca municipality at both the Convention of 1833 and the Consultation of 1835 where the General Council of the provisional state government appointed Silas as the first Texas Ranger in the North Texas area. The twenty-five men under his command were to range between the Brazos and Trinity Rivers protecting the frontier settlers from hostile Indians. During the Texas Revolution everyone at Parker's Fort joined the panic civilian retreat known as the Runaway Scrape and fled to the Trinity only to be stopped by flood waters. While camped there they heard news of Sam Houston's victory over Santa Anna in the Battle of San Jacinto, so they quickly returned to their stockade and disbanded the Ranger force.

After the Texian victory over the Mexican army, it

70

was only natural for the Parker family to relax, lower their guard, and be lulled into a false and deadly sense of security. There were only six men inside Fort Parker at nine o'clock on the morning of May 19, 1836, when some five hundred Comanche, Kiowa and Caddo warriors approached the open fort gate carrying a soiled white flag; they asked directions to a water hole and requested that a beef be given them. When Benjamin Parker went outside the gate to palaver, he was speared to death and the massacre was on. Brother Silas, who was guarding the gate, was the next to die as he tried to save the life of his niece, Mrs. Rachel Plummer. Samuel Frost and son Robert were killed inside but Elder John Parker and his wife escaped out the back door of the fort, only to be overtaken after three-quarters of a mile; his scalp was taken and his genitals ripped off before he was killed while Granny Parker was penned to the ground with a lance, stripped and raped by several Indians before being left for dead. In all, five white men were killed during the attack and two women later died of their wounds while the rest of the Parker clan fled to the safety of the Navasota bottoms. When L.M.S. Plummer returned to the fort and learned that his wife and son had been taken captive, he spent the next six days wandering aimlessly in the woods, armed only with a butcher knife as he searched for his lost loved ones. In the meantime James Parker led the eighteen survivors on a ninety-mile, six-day march to Fort Houston, located two miles south of present Palestine. Most of these pathetic marchers were women and children, ranging in ages from one to twelve, and their only food supply en route was two skunks and two turtles. Many of the young ones wore only shirts but no pants or shoes so the thick, tangled briars and brambles left their feet and legs torn and bloody. Finally the desperate Parker struck out alone, made the last thirty-five miles in an incredible eight hours, and sent a detail of twelve soldiers to bury the dead at Fort Parker.

71

The Indian war party had plundered the fort, then retreated northwest with their five white captives tied to ponies. The victims were James Parker's married daughter, Mrs. Rachel Plummer, and her two-year-old son James Pratt along with a young married woman, Mrs. Elizabeth Kellogg, and two children of Silas Parker, nine-year-old Cynthia Ann and six-year-old John. When the raiders stopped at midnight to hold a victory dance on an open prairie, Cynthia Ann recognized the scalps of her father and grandfather dangling from warrior belts. All of the captives were denied food and had their hands and feet tied before being thrown on their faces. They were then stomped on and beaten bloody with bows; the two white women were also stripped, tortured and raped throughout the night.

At daybreak the Comanches and Kiowas headed west with Mrs. Plummer and the three children while the Caddoes carried Mrs. Kellogg with them. After keeping her for six months, they traded Elizabeth to the Delawares, who in December 1836 sold her to General Sam Houston for $150 at Nacogdoches. Mrs. Plummer, however, was not to be so fortunate. When the Comanches finally made camp in northeastern Colorado, she became a warrior's slave for eighteen months, performing the most menial tasks and becoming as lice-infested and filthy as the other women. During the day she dressed buffalo skins; at night she minded the horses. Life in the snow-covered high mountains left her bare feet frostbitten. In October 1836 Rachel gave birth to a beautiful, healthy second son but when he was six months old, her "master" decided that the child interfered with her work. An Indian brave then tore the sucking babe from Rachel's breast, strangled him, then repeatedly tossed the infant into the air and allowed him to fall on the frozen ground until life seemed extinct. However, the battered boy revived and began to breathe again after mother washed the blood from its face. Seeing this the Indians tied a rope around his neck and dragged the baby through a bunch of prickly pears, literally ripping the flesh from its body. A mounted brave then tied the rope to his saddle and galloped around until the child was bounced and torn to pieces; only then was Rachel allowed to gather up and bury the remains. After some Comancheros traded for her in the foothills of the Rockies, Mrs. Plummer was eventually ransomed by a Santa Fe merchant, William Donahue, who took her to Independence, Missouri, where a brother-in-law, L.S. Nixon, escorted Rachel back to Texas. This "soiled" lady was to face shame and humiliation upon returning to her father's home on February 19, 1838, and died exactly one year later after writing a narrative about her ordeal. Rachel's son, James Pratt, was ransomed back after six years of captivity and taken to Fort Gibson in 1842. He was back home in February 1843 and returned to a normal life as a resident of Anderson County.

And what of the Parker children? John was located and ransomed in 1842 but returned to the Comanches at his mother's request to seek his sister. After accompanying a raiding party into Mexico, he fell in love with Dona Juanita, a beautiful captive Mexican girl of Aztec descent. On the return trip in the Llano Estacado, John developed smallpox and the Indians deserted him but his newfound love nursed and cheered him back to health. In 1845 the Texas legislature voted $300 in an unsuccessful attempt to find him; by this time John had become a stockman and rancher in the desert below the Rio Grande and was said to look like a typical Indian. During the Civil War he joined a Mexican company of the Confederate army but refused to serve outside Texas. He would never again visit any of his white relatives and died in Mexico in 1915.

Cynthia Ann was taken by a band of Kwahadi (Antelope Eater) Comanches who ranged the high "Staked Plain" of the Texas Panhandle. She went by the Indian

73

name of "Naduah," living at first with an old squaw and learning the language and customs of a people who considered women as beasts of burden. While the men sat in council, hunted and raided, the squaws set up the tee-pees, loaded pack mules, dressed skins, and cooked meat. Naduah also had to adapt to radically different eating and drinking habits. The Kwahadis drank the warm blood of freshly killed buffalo and deer while raw brains and bone marrow were a favorite meat sauce. They were fond of warm liver, gall bladder bile, warm stripped entrails, and the milk-and-blood mixture from a buffalo udder. These Indians considered fish taboo because of their odor and were not cannibalistic. The Kwahadis had bright copper-colored skin, black hair and eyes, and thin lips. The men tended to be short and heavy and wore moccasins, leggings and a breech-cloth. The women looked ugly and prematurely aged and wore gowns from chin to ankle. Naduah was to spend twenty-five years with this culture and came to love and appreciate Comanche life.

While in her teens the blue-eyed, blonde-haired Cynthia Ann became the bride of Nokoni war chief Peta Nacona. In 1847 she gave birth to their first son, Quanah, which means "sweet odor" or "fragrant" in Comanche. He learned to ride before he could walk, had his first pony at age five, went on his first raid and killed his first enemy at age fifteen, and was a war chief in his twenties. When Quanah was a maturing boy, his mother had another son, Pecos, and then a daughter named Prairie Flower or Topsannah. Chief Peta Nacona loved his white wife and, contrary to custom, took no others.

For years there was no word of Cynthia Ann; then in 1846 a federal agent, Colonel Leonard Williams, saw her at an Indian council on the Canadian River but she would say nothing, began to cry, and ran away to hide. When Williams offered twelve mules and two loads of merchandise for her, he was refused, threatened with death, and received a fierce look from old band chief Pa-ha-u-ka. On November 18, 1847, Indian agent Colonel Robert Neighbors again reported seeing Cynthia. Randolph B. Marcy spoke of her in his 1852 book, *Exploration of the Red River*, saying that neither he nor her ransomed brother John could persuade her to leave the Indians. Some years after her capture, Victor M. Rose accompanied a party of white hunters that visited a Comanche camp on the upper Canadian; when he recognized and questioned Naduah, she said, "I am happily wedded. I love my husband, who is good and kind, and my little ones who, too, are his, and I can not forsake them!" The first recorded mention of her husband came in March 1858 at the Battle of Antelope Hills on the Canadian River in present Oklahoma. With Cynthia Ann as a bystander, a force of 500 warriors led by Chief Nacona was defeated and forced to retreat by the superior firepower of 221 Texas Rangers and Tonkawa Indians led by Colonel John S. "Rip" Ford and Chief Placido; seventy-five Comanches were killed in the encounter while only two Rangers were lost.

In the fall of 1860, Peta Nacona led a raid through Parker County, named in honor of his wife's uncle Isaac, as far west as Weatherford. Governor Sam Houston then appointed Ranger Captain Sul Ross to hunt down and destroy these Comanches. When Ross left Camp Cooper forty miles west of Fort Belknap, he had a force of forty Rangers, twenty soldiers from the Second Cavalry, and seventy volunteer cowboys led by Jack Cureton. They rode for several days before hearing the sounds of ravens; these birds were attracted by blood and raw meat so Ross knew that Indian buffalo hunters were nearby. On December 18, 1860, a clash known as the Battle of Pease River or the Ross Raid took place when the Texans came upon a detached Comanche hunting camp beneath the cliffs of the Pease River Valley, a place that offered a shield against the seasonal blue northers. A sandstorm kept Ross and his men hidden from view so the Indians were totally unprepared for the sudden attack. At the time, all of the warriors, including Peta Nacona and his two sons, were miles away looking for a new campsite so the camp was occupied only by unarmed women, children, and some Mexican slaves drying meat for the winter. The result was really a massacre rather than a battle: one man was killed with the rest of the victims being women; the surviving women and children were routed and scattered. During the charge Captain Ross killed a Mexican slave known as Nacona's Joe but thought his victim was in fact Chief Nacona.[1] In the midst of the melee, a Lieutenant Kelliheir chased an "old squaw" rider holding a baby in arms which turned out to be the thirty-four-year-old Cynthia Ann and her two-year-old daughter, Prairie Flower. Their lives were probably saved by scout Charles Goodnight, who noticed her dirty, dung-greased blonde hair and shouted, "Don't shoot — That's a white woman." Although she had hard, coarse facial lines and a dirty unkempt appearance, Captain Ross observed Cynthia Ann's blue eyes and agreed that she was white.

After crying all that first night, the "rescued"

---

1. Ross later claimed that he chased Nacona and a teenage girl mounted behind him for about a mile and a half; when his pistol shot killed the young girl, her dead weight also pulled the chief off his horse. At that very moment the Ranger's mount was hit by one of Peta's arrows and started to buck wildly. While he was clinging to the pommel of his saddle, a random shot from Ross's pistol shattered the Indian's right arm at the elbow. Once his horse calmed down, Sul shot the chief twice more through the body, prompting Nacona to struggle to a nearby small tree and start chanting a wild, wierd death song. The Ranger's appeal to surrender was answered by a defiant but errant thrust of the lance in Peta's left hand. Although his hopeless situation caused Ross to look on him with pity and admiration, the chief seemed to prefer death to life so the Ranger captain ordered his Mexican servant and interpreter to "end his misery by a charge of buckshot." Ross then sent his accoutrements to Governor Houston to be deposited in the archives at Austin. This version of the death of Peta Nacona was later vehemently denied by the chief's eldest son, Quanah Parker, in a 1910 Dallas speech.

mother and daughter were taken to Camp Cooper on the Clear Fork of the Brazos River where they were attended by Mrs. Evans, wife of the commandant, and the other ladies. Ross also sent word to have former State Senator Isaac Parker come and try to identify her. At first her uncle's questions brought only a blank stare and Parker finally said, "Maybe we are wrong — poor Cynthia Ann." After hearing those words she pressed her hand over her heart, broke into tears, and said, "Cynthia — me Cynthia." She and Prairie Flower were then taken to Isaac's home at Birdville in Tarrant County, where the bewildered mother was reintroduced to a forgotten culture.[2] For several months she continued to eat with her fingers and preferred to sleep on the floor rather than in a bed.

She was taken to the secession convention meeting at Austin where Mrs. John Henry Brown and Mrs. N.C. Raymond dressed her neatly and took Cynthia Ann to the gallery of the convention hall. However, these spectators quickly left when she became frightened, thinking it was a council of chiefs deciding on her life. On April 8, 1861, the state legislature passed a law granting her a pension of $1000 a year for five years and a league of land (4,428 acres). When Cynthia visited Fort Worth in 1862, A.F. Corning took her to a deguerreotype gallery and persuaded her to have her picture taken holding Prairie Flower, the only likeness of her that exists. By then she had cut off her long hair in the Comanche mourning tradition. The original was exhibited for years at the Academy of Art in Waco and is now in the library of Baylor University. In 1874 her son Quanah advertised in the *Fort Worth Gazette* for a picture of his long-lost mother, prompting Sul Ross, then living at Waco, to forward him a copy. The cattleman Burk Burnett later had

2. In April 1939 Amon G. Carter of Fort Worth moved this double log cabin, rebuilt it on his Lake Worth country estate, "Shady Oaks," and named it "Cynthia Ann's House." It is now open to the public and stands in the Log Cabin Village in a Fort Worth city park.

it copied in oil so the proud Parker could display the portrait on the walls of his home at Cache, Oklahoma.

In 1862 Cynthia Ann moved to the home of her brother, Silas Parker Jr., in Van Zandt County. During the Civil War she learned English and such domestic duties as spinning cloth, plaiting rugs, churning and cooking. She never smiled in her last lonely years. Separated from her two boys, she feared that they were lost on the prairie and would starve to death; three times she tried to run away in hopes of finding them and had to be put under guard. She would take a knife, hack her breasts, put the blood on tobacco, and burn it as she cried for her lost boys. Relatives often saw Cynthia Ann sitting on the front porch, rocking her daughter and weeping. When her little Prairie Flower died of a fever in 1864, the grieving, heartbroken mother moved to the home of her brother-in-law, Ruff O'Quinn, in Anderson County. There she mutilated herself, cried, howled, refused to eat for a time, and then became even more docile, moody and silent. When she died in 1871, mother and daughter were buried together in the Foster Cemetery south of Poynor; in 1965 a State Historical Marker was placed at the site.

And what of her husband and two sons? Peta Nacona never took another woman and died of an infected wound in 1864 while hunting plums on the Canadian River. Pecos (or Peanut) soon died of disease on the plains while the half-breed named Quanah in his twenties became the legendary last war chief of the Kwahadi band of Comanches. Texans would soon be fearing and hating this young warrior.

During and after the Civil War, the Comanches and Kiowas roamed at will throughout Central Texas. The country west of a line drawn from Gainesville to Fredericksburg was practically abandoned by settlers while only one-fifth of the ranches in the Waco area were still occupied by April 1866. Such Indian depredations caused the United States Congress to call for a grand peace council with the south plains Indians at Medicine Lodge Creek, Kansas in 1867. That October ten Comanche chiefs who were present signed a treaty which set up a three million acre reservation for Comanches and Kiowas in present southwestern Oklahoma. The Kwahadis, however, sent no representatives to this council. Quanah opposed the treaty and refused to sign it, saying that his band were warriors and would not live on a reservation. It is noteworthy that some warriors were already refusing to join him on raids since he did not share freely, tending instead to keep the best horses for himself or for favorite relatives. Such a selfish leader lost prestige since keeping the bulk of the spoils showed waning power and fear of being unable to get more.

In 1870 the War Department transferred Colonel Ranald Mackenzie and his tough Fourth Cavalry to the Texas frontier to stop raids by off-reservation Indians. During the Civil War General Ulysses S. Grant had called Mackenzie "the most promising young officer in the army." In October 1871 he led 600 troops northwest into the Llano Estacado, aiming to punish Quanah and his Kwahadi band for their theft of thousands of Texas horses and cattle. As his men advanced onto the high grass prairies, Mackenzie was frustrated by the Comanche tactic of never giving battle or presenting bunched targets; they would instead make sudden attacks on camps and picket lines, killing sentries and stampeding horses. When pressed, Quanah's warriors swerved away from charges and melted into the plains. Cavalry troops, on the other hand, had been trained to fight as units using mass tactics, not to engage in individual horse-to-horse engagements. The final embarrassment came around midnight on October 10 when Quanah led a charge through the army camp ringing cowbells and flapping buffalo skins to panic the cavalry horses; in the resulting stampede he captured sixty-six horses including Mackenzie's own prize mount. A blizzard two days later forced the chagrined colonel to call off the chase. When he returned to Fort Richardson on a litter, all he had to show for his first encounter with Quanah was an arrow embedded in his hip. He had failed either to catch or punish the Kwahadis, who simply retreated higher into the Llano Estacado.

The next mention of Quanah in written records was as the leader in the Battle of Adobe Walls. By terms of the Treaty of Medicine Lodge Creek, no white buffalo hunters were to be allowed south of the Arkansas River, the so-called "Dead Line." The treaty thus created a buffalo hunting preserve for Indians only in the Texas Panhandle but the promise was ignored by the U.S. Army in the 1870s; in fact, General Phil Sheridan, Commander of the Military Department of the Southwest, praised trespassing hunters for solving "the vexed Indian question" by destroying "the Indians' commissary." In his view slaughtering the buffalo would starve Indians off the plains and force them to reservations and government rations. Since the army was giving its tacit approval and with the northern herd almost gone, a young buffalo hunter named Billy Dixon left Dodge City in the fall of 1873 to look over the Panhandle range. By early June 1874 twenty-eight buffalo hunters and one woman built a stockade of three picket or sod houses on the South Canadian River sixty miles northeast of present Amarillo. The houses fronted a path on a straight line with little thought given to defense. Their base was a mile from the ruins of a deserted trading post called Adobe Walls, built by Colonel William Bent about 1844. At this time they began to decimate a huge buffalo herd moving north from its Texas wintering grounds. These hunters would soon face the wrath of the largest Indian war party ever assembled on the south plains.

During that spring of 1874, heavy rains prevented freight wagons from reaching the Kiowa–Comanche reservation, forcing the agent at Fort Sill to issue half rations. By then, restive young warriors were coming to the reservation only occasionally and often found no sugar or coffee, mouldy meal and flour, rotten tobacco and tough, inferior beef. This new problem of food shortages made these younger braves receptive to the preachings of an adolescent Kwahadi medicine man named Isa-Tai (or wolf droppings), who claimed to be a prophet and to have had communion with the Great Spirit. Isa-Tai boasted that he could belch up wagonloads of cartridges and that his magic paint would protect warriors and horses from bullets. After he predicted that a comet would last five days and would be followed by a summer-long drought, both events transpired. He was also grieving and seeking revenge because white men had recently killed his uncle in a Texas battle. Thus an immediate goal was the recruiting of a large war party and Quanah Parker became an early, fervent convert and recruit. In May, Isa-Tai sent out runners requesting all Comanche bands to attend and perform their first sacred Sun Dance near the reservation boundary. During the three-day war council, the Kiowas, Kiowa–Apaches, Cheyennes and Arapahos were invited to join the war party. After much whiskey flowed and Isa-Tai staged a mystical display of magic, Quanah was chosen as paramount war chief with his first target being the white buffalo hunters in the Texas Panhandle.

On the night of June 26, 1874, Quanah and five tribes of 700 Indians reached Adobe Walls. That same evening brothers Ike and Shorty Shadler arrived there with a wagonload of goods, parked on the north side of the corral near Myers's store, and bedded down under their wagon. Amos Chapman, an army scout from Camp Supply, had earlier warned saloon owner Jim Hanrahan that a massive Indian attack would come the morning after the next full moon, Saturday, June 27. Chapman had gathered this intelligence after some Penateka Comanches at Fort Sill had told of the war council. At first

Hanrahan kept the secret to himself, fearing that all his alarmed customers, the buffalo hunters, might pack up and leave. Finally his conscience got the best of him and at 2:00 A.M. on June 27, Hanrahan shot his pistol into the air and shouted, "Clear out! The ridgepole is breaking!" The loud cracking noise was really a trick; there was no damage at all but the "repairs" on the saloon roof took two hours and Hanrahan then served drinks "on the house" to keep everyone awake until dawn. Billy Dixon had intended to get an early hunting start that morning and was thus the first to see the huge Indian war party in the tree line by the creek; in fact, he and nineteen-year-old Bat Masterson barely made it into Hanrahan's saloon just ahead of the charging savages. The buffalo hunters frantically holed up in the three large buildings and barricaded the doors and windows with grain and flour sacks. During the battle that followed, they were isolated from each other and could communicate only by shouting.

Quanah Parker led the first Indian charge with Kwahadi and Cheyenne braves close behind while Isa-Tai sat naked watching from a distant butte, wearing only his coat of magic yellow war paint. Quanah first tried to break down a cabin door by backing his pony into it and battering it with his rifle stock but the door held firm. When he saw a companion shot at the door of a building, Parker carried him to safety, clinging to his horse by only an arm and a foot. Just before noon his pony was shot from under him, pitching Quanah to the ground. After scurrying to the shelter of a rotten buffalo carcass, a ball struck him between the neck and shoulder blade, leaving an arm paralyzed for hours, but he managed to drag himself to a plum thicket and lay there until rescued by another horseman.

During the initial Indian charge, the Shadler brothers were riddled with arrows and bullets and scalped while asleep under their wagon. Their big black labrador defended his masters so viciously that the warriors counted coup on and cut a fur "scalp" from the brave dog's side. In the early hours of the attack, the Indian charges were directed by the bugle calls of a deserter from the all-black Tenth Cavalry at Fort Sill. However, he was shot in the back and killed while looting the Shadler wagon of coffee and sugar. The white defenders were left on foot early on when all of their fifty-six horses and twenty-eight oxen were killed. Although vastly outnumbered they did have two great advantages: they were crack marksmen and armed with the .50 caliber Sharps "Big Fifty" rifle, an accurate and long-range weapon. This firepower edge became even more decisive when the attackers made a fatal error by splitting around the walls and circling the buildings at full gallop rather than making a mass charge at close quarters. Thirteen Indian corpses were left near the cabins when the actual fighting ended around noon and the attackers withdrew to the distant ridges carrying off fifteen more of their dead.

At this point the Battle of Adobe Walls turned into a five-day siege in which Indian carbines were no match for the "Big Fifty" buffalo guns firing at a distance. On the second day the white hunters were able to drag the stinking horse carcasses off to a burial pit. During a war council on a butte, Isa-Tai's pony was hit in the forehead by a "Big Fifty" ball and dropped dead in his tracks although covered with the magic war paint. His medicine was obviously flawed so an enraged Cheyenne brave named "Hippy" began to beat Isa-Tai with his quirt until some older chiefs stopped him. On the third day of the siege, Billy Dixon got off his famous "mile long shot" by knocking a Cheyenne off his horse on a bluff 1,538 yards away, stunning but not killing him. This brave had been beside the awed Isa-Tai who remarked, "The whites . . . shoot today, maybe so kill you tomorrow." This miraculous Dixon shot ended the battle and the disgraced medicine man later alibied that a Cheyenne had destroyed his medicine the day before the assault by violating a taboo and killing a skunk. No wonder that Isa-Tai is known in Comanche tradition as "that comical fellow."

By the time the Indians withdrew on the fifth day, news of the attack caused one hundred white hunters to gather at Adobe Walls. The defenders had suffered only three losses but were in a vengeful mood when they decapitated the thirteen dead Indians and stuck their heads on the sharpened posts of the corral gate. After the last of the hunters departed on August 20, the Indians destroyed the vacant buildings. Adobe Walls was a crippling defeat for the Indians, who probably had at least seventy warriors killed or wounded and saw their fragile alliance shattered. However, the discredited medicine man was blamed for the loss rather than Quanah.

The attack did break up buffalo hunting in the Texas Panhandle. Billy Dixon never hunted again, joined the U.S. Army as a scout, and served until February 1883. When he revisited the ruins of Adobe Walls in the fall of 1874, Billy found his dog "Fanny" and her four pups, the last survivors of the battle. Years later he and Quanah met, shook hands, and discussed the fight; it may have been at this time when Parker summed up the outcome by saying, "No use Indians fight Adobe."

The end of an Indian way of life was near when Colonel Mackenzie led a 600-man Fourth Cavalry "Southern Column" from Fort Concho north into the Kwahadi Panhandle stronghold in September 1874. He had orders to "break up their camps," knowing that the one great Comanche vulnerability was their practice of carrying women, children, and supplies with them. This was strictly a regular army campaign with the infantrymen riding in mule-drawn wagons. Mackenzie was able to find Quanah only by capturing a despised half-breed Comanchero named Jose Piedad Tafoya, who had traded with the Comanches for nine years and knew the location of their great hidden camp in Palo Duro Canyon. Tafoya told of the hideout after his neck was stretched on the high end of a propped-up wagon tongue. When Charles Goodnight told Parker of this betrayal four years later, the livid chief vowed that "if he ever laid eyes on Tofoya, he would broil him in the fire."

On September 27, 1874, Sergeant John Charlton and two Tonkawa scouts peered over the lip of the huge crevasse known as Palo Duro Canyon; below them were two miles of Comanche, Kiowa, and Cheyenne teepees strung out along the winding Prairie Dog Town Fork of the Red River. The three then rode back the twenty-five miles to Mackenzie's camp in Tule Canyon where the colonel left his supply wagons behind and ordered an all-night cavalry march. After reaching the canyon rim at dawn on September 28, the scouts found one trail to the canyon floor, a path so narrow that the soldiers had to dismount and scramble down leading their horses in single file. When they were 150 yards down, an Indian sentry spotted them and gave the alarm with a war whoop, rifle shot, and by waving a red blanket; nevertheless almost all the braves were caught unawares in their teepees so Colonel Eugene Beaumont's "A" Company was able to dash two miles straight up the canyon and return with 1,424 captured Indian ponies.

Due to the slow movement of Mackenzie's troops to the canyon bottom, they were unable to attack in force, allowing the warriors to resist long enough for their women and children to retreat and scramble up the canyon walls; then the men escaped and scattered. Only four Indians and no troopers were killed in the Battle of Palo Duro Canyon but Mackenzie accomplished his objective by destroying food, property and morale. He first burned a huge cache of supplies including tons of calico, flour, sugar, blankets and cured buffalo meat along with crates of new carbines, ammunition, and lead and powder kegs. Knowing that the Comanches were helpless on foot, Mackenzie took 350 of the captured ponies for his scouts and men, then ordered the rest driven to Tule Canyon

85

and shot. For years the execution site was marked by a huge pile of bleached bones until they were hauled away and sold for fertilizer. The ruthless strategy worked: during the winter of 1874–1875, groups of Indians straggled into Fort Sill to surrender and accept rations. Kiowa leader Lone Wolf and the worst of the war chiefs were exiled to Fort Marion, Florida, under military guard. All the Indians were disarmed and the most dangerous warriors were placed in an unfinished ice house where they were thrown raw meat.

At the time of the Palo Duro attack, Quanah was far to the south so he and 400 of his Kwahadi band had enough horses to hold out and move deeper into the Llano Estacado. Many of them froze and starved that winter while others survived on rodents, grubs and nuts. In late April 1875 Mackenzie, who was then in command at Fort Sill, sent Dr. J.J. Sturm to seek out Quanah and lay down conditions of surrender. After traveling for days Dr. Sturm found Parker on the western side of the Staked Plain and described him as "a young man of much influence." Quanah was offered safety and good treatment if he would come to the reservation; if he held out, "Kinzie" would hunt down and exterminate his band. After three days of debate, medicine man Isa-Tai made the decision to head for Fort Sill rather than face starvation on the buffalo-less plains. On June 2, 1875, Chief Parker led a column of 400 warriors and 2,000 ponies into Fort Sill to meet his great enemy face to face. He thus became the last of the south plains Indian chiefs to surrender.

Since he had never sat down with the white man or broken treaties or promises, Quanah was not treated harshly. He had served his people before in war; now he would serve them in subjugation. After first making him band chief in 1875, Mackenzie with Washington's consent made the half-breed principal chief of *all* the Comanches; this had never been done before but the federal government and the army wanted *one* Indian leader to deal with. Parker was the last Comanche to bear this title and even ordered the term put on his stationery heading. The choice proved to be a wise one with Quanah being useful, diplomatic, and deferential in the exercise of his power. In the summer of 1877, he brought in twenty-one runaways and persuaded Mackenzie to be lenient with them. While attending a general Indian council in 1881, he was heard to remark, "I am young and almost a boy, talking for assistance for my people." During the same council he wrote a note to Agent P.B. Hunt and said, "Even though I am here with my friends, yet there is but one council [sic] I listen to, and that is yours." In April 1887 the Kiowas asked Quanah to join them in attacking Fort Sill; in reporting the proposal to Agent Hall, he said, "Me and my people have quit fighting long ago and we have no desire to join anyone in war again."

The transition to reservation life was difficult for the nomadic Comanches, who had never planted seed in all their history but were now expected to farm. On a typical ration or Issue Day every two weeks, they were given a poor 500-pound steer to provide meat for twenty-five Indians along with a ration of coffee, sugar, flour, rice and salt which was less than half that of a soldier. In the fall of 1878, a sympathetic new agent, P.B. Hunt, arranged passes for all of the beef-hungry tribe to leave the reservation for a buffalo hunt. Some 1500 joyful Indians and a small military escort started out in an expectant mood but they saw only bones as they headed west. When the snow came and their supplies ran out, Agent Hunt sent wagons of food to the disappointed, starving hunters but Quanah continued his search, leading a party to Palo Duro Canyon where Charles Goodnight had founded the JA Ranch. During that severe winter of 1878, JA cowhands reported that Indians were killing their cattle at "a fearful rate." Goodnight met with Parker and the two made a treaty whereby the rancher gave the Comanches two beeves a day to eat on condition that they not disturb his herd. Charles always considered Quanah a friend after this encounter and later gave him a Durham bull. In the spring of 1879, a company of black cavalry from Fort Elliott escorted the stragglers back to the reservation.

Upon his arrival at Fort Sill, Quanah told Colonel Mackenzie of his white mother and asked for help in locating her. As a result of letters written to Texas army installations and newspaper publicity, a Parker family member informed the colonel that Cynthia Ann was dead. After taking the "white man's road," the chief became more interested in his mother's story and adopted the Parker name for his own. The Indian agent even gave him an introductory letter and permission to come alone to Texas and visit his mother's family. After he located her brother Silas in East Texas, the Parkers made him welcome, helped him with his English, and taught him farm tasks. Quanah also went to Chihuahua, Mexico, to visit his uncle John and brought peyote back to the reservation upon his return. At first he thought the bitter-tasting "buttons" of the peyote cactus had curative powers but later favored the ceremonial use of this hallucinogenic drug as an escape from the reality of reservation life. Parker and the Comanches would eat these buttons in all-night rites and they brought a sense of euphoria, peace, relaxation and spiritual communion with other users. Although the buttons were not addictive, some Indian agents compared them to opium and made an issue of the peyote culture in the late 1880s. Even so, the Comanches were committed to peyote (mescal) as a highly ceremonial form of religion by 1890.

From 1886 until the reservation was dissolved in 1901, Quanah served as chief judge of the three-man Court of Indian Offenses. They were chosen from the three tribes (Comanche, Kiowa, and Kiowa–Apache) with the approval of the agent and had the power to try such minor offenses as the holding of sun and scalp dances, polygamy, medicine making, timber selling, fighting, stealing and selling girls. If the party was found guilty, the judges could assess fines and jail sentences.

Chief Parker was quick to adapt to the life of a cattleman. Since the Texas cattle trails went through Indian Territory to the Kansas railheads, he received permission from the Indian agent to charge a dollar a head for cattle crossing reservation land. However, his most lucrative business was that of leasing grazing rights to the three million acres making up the Kiowa–Comanche reservation. For three years some North Texas cattlemen grazed their herds on these lands as illegal intruders; then in February 1885, the federal government authorized six-year leases of 1.5 million acres of reservation land at an annual rent of six cents an acre. That summer the Comanches shared in their first semi-annual "grass payments" of $9.50 each for their southern part of the reservation. During the life of this lease, the three tribes received an annual income of about $55,000. Quanah also had his own private pasture of 44,000 acres which he leased to such rich Texas cattlemen as Samuel Burk Burnett and W. T. Waggoner for $100,000 a year. In June 1890 Parker traveled to Washington, D.C., to lobby for the leases which were renewed in 1891 but limited to one-year periods. Since the grazing leases also required the approval of the Commissioner of Indian Affairs, he made many subsequent trips to the capital where he also promoted Indian rights in Congress.

Burk Burnett also advised Quanah on investments and built him a showplace twelve-room, $2,000 ranchhouse near Cache, Oklahoma. Known locally as the Comanche White House (or Star House), it had a two-story porch around three sides and was painted white with twenty-two white stars on a red roof. The house contained separate bedrooms for each of his three wives and was surrounded by a tall picket fence. Among the notables entertained there was Lord Bryce, the English ambassador. Texas cattle barons also gifted Parker with diamond stickpins, fine suits, a $1,000 carriage, engraved pearl-handled revolvers, and trips to Fort Worth. On December 19, 1885, he took his uncle by marriage, old Chief Yellow Bear, along for company on one such visit. After arriving on the Fort Worth & Denver railroad, the two were assigned the most expensive suite in the elegant, new Pickwick Hotel. However, Yellow Bear had no use for plush, fancy beds and insisted on sleeping on a blanket on the floor. He turned in about ten o'clock and legend has it that since the lights bothered him, he blew out the flickering gas lamp light and went to sleep quickly — and permanently. The story goes that Parker came back to the room about midnight and scrambled into bed without smelling the deadly gas. When the two Indians failed to appear at breakfast or dinner the next day, the alarmed hotel clerk sent a man to awaken them. Yellow Bear was found dead in a crouched position with his face pressed to the floor; the unconscious Quanah was discovered flat on his back by a closed window but Doctors Beall and Moore managed to revive him. In an interview with the *Fort Worth Evening Mail*, the sheepish Parker later admitted that he was responsible for his uncle's death. It seems that he had gone out for a night on the town and failed to turn off the gas lamp valve completely when he turned in. Although he was awakened by coal gas fumes, he felt too "sick" and "crazy" to realize that they were lethal; in fact, the last thing he remembered was getting up and falling down "all around the room."

On February 4, 1886, Quanah received some visitors while he and a thousand of his "subjects" were camped in some foothills near Anadarko. He had three squaws at the time with his favorite being the daughter of Yellow Bear; Parker boasted of having given seventeen horses for her! Cynthia, one of his daughters and the namesake of her white grandmother, was living in the Indian agent's house. After a visit in his teepee, one of the visitors wrote a letter and described Quanah as follows:

> He is a fine specimen of physical manhood, tall, muscular, as straight as an arrow, . . . very dark skin, perfect teeth, and heavy, raven black hair . . . hanging in two rolls wrapped around with red cloth . . .
>
> . . . Quanah was attired in a full suit of buckskin, tunic, leggings and moccasins elaborately trimmed in beads, a red breech cloth with ornamental ends hanging down. A very handsome and expensive Mexican blanket was thrown around his body; in his ears were little stuffed birds. His hair was done with the feathers of bright plumaged birds . . . His general aspect, manner, bearing, education, natural intelligence show plainly that white blood trickles through his veins . . . He has a handsome carriage, drives a pair of matched grays, always traveling with one of his squaws (to do the chores). Minna-a-ton-cha is with him now. She knows no English, but while her lord is conversing gazes dumb with admiration at 'my Lord' ready to obey his slightest wish or command.

In 1886 a town halfway between the Red and Pease Rivers was named for him so Quanah went there to make a speech of thanks; in fact, he invested $40,000 to become the major stockholder in the Quanah, Acme and Pacific Railroad running through his namesake. Whenever he traveled to Fort Worth, Dallas, or Washington on business, he wore a regular black business suit with a gold watch and chain dangling from his vest pocket, a black felt derby hat, and regular "toothpick" dude shoes. It is no wonder that he was such good newspaper copy and so sought after by promoters of parades and town celebrations. Although he was obviously successful in adapting to the white man's ways, he could also lecture him in blunt language; speaking to a white audience in a Fourth of July speech in 1898, Quanah remarked, "We fear your success. This was a pretty country you took away from us but you see how dry it is now. It is only good for red ants, coyotes, and cattlemen."

On June 6, 1900, the United States Congress enacted the so-called Jerome Agreement into law, ending Quanah's financial heyday and opening the Kiowa–Comanche reservation to white settlement. The act provided that each Indian man, woman and child was to select 160 acres of land while 414,720 acres of land fronting on the Red River (the "Big Pasture") was to be held in common by the three tribes. The Indians were to surrender rights to all other reservation lands in return for $500,000; these lands were to be surveyed into homesteads of 160 acres each and thrown open to the public by lottery rather than by "run." However, even the "Big Pasture" reserve lands were opened to sale in June 1906 at which time the Comanches lost their grazing leases and the last of their tribal land holdings.

After first meeting Theodore Roosevelt at a reunion of his Rough Riders at Oklahoma City, the celebrated Chief Parker seemed a logical choice to serve as one of five tribesmen riding in Roosevelt's Inaugural Parade in 1905. A month later Quanah was invited to be the honored guest when President Roosevelt went on a publicized wolf hunt in the Big Pasture of the Kiowa–Comanche reservation; at Anadarko T.R. even summoned the chief to his side. After watching Jack Abernathy catch wolves with his bare hands by day, Roosevelt was entertained by Quanah's campfire tales each night. A touchy situation developed, however, when three of Parker's wives arrived on the second day of the hunt. When Roosevelt at the first opportunity urged him to mend his ways and keep only one wife, Quanah replied, "*You* tell them which one I keep."

After 1906 Parker served as liaison between the federal government and his tribe. Like other bureaucrats he drew a per diem for his frequent trips to Anadarko and even had a telephone installed in his Star House at government expense. During this period an investigator sent from Washington to check on the peyote and polygamy issues said of him:

> If ever Nature stamped a man with the seal of headship she did it in his case. Quanah would have been a leader and a governor in any circle where fate may have cast him — it is in his blood.

Cattleman Burnett often arranged for Quanah to lead Indian parades at the Fort Worth Fat Stock Show. While being entertained on Burnett property near Vernon, Texas, in 1909, he was informed that he must buy a license to hunt; the incredulous chief fired off a protest letter to the governor in which he said, "I am Texas man myself." During a feature speech at the Texas State Fair at Dallas in 1910, Parker chose to set the record straight about the death of his father, Peta Nacona, by noting:

> The history books say General Ross kill my father. This damn lie . . . He not there. After the fight at Mule Creek (junction with Pease River) — two, three, maybe four years — my father sick. I see him die. I want to get that in Texas history — straight up.

At first Quanah sent his own children to the Fort Sill School. In 1906 he enrolled a son in the Cache public schools but the boy was denied readmission the next year because his father lived outside the school district. Parker then took the lead in forming a new school district for Comanche country which included his home. When this school started in September 1908, the old chief was elected as president of the school board. Four of his children were among the first Comanches to attend the Carlisle Indian School in Pennsylvania. His eight marriages produced twenty-five children; one son, White Parker, became a Methodist minister to the Comanches while two daughters married white cattlemen.

In his twilight years Quanah's final goal was to bring his mother's remains back to the reservation for burial. In 1908 he located the site of her grave by run-

93

ning advertisements in Texas newspapers. Texan resistance to his objective was softened when he wrote a moving letter that was read to the churches of East Texas. It read in part:

> My mother. She fed me. She held me. She carried me in her arms . . . I cry, she sad . . . I sick, she awake. I thirsty, she get water . . . I want, she get . . . They took my mother away. They kept her. They would not let me see her. Now she dead. Her boy want to bury her.

After he persuaded Texas Congressman John Stephens to sponsor such legislation, Congress in March 1909 appropriated $1,000 for a monument to Cynthia Ann Parker and in June 1910 voted $800 to finance her reburial. A.C. Birdsong, a rancher at Cache and the husband of Quanah's daughter, Laura Neda Parker, located and identified the remains of Cynthia Ann, finding that Prairie Flower was buried with her. After he brought the two back to the Ritter Funeral Home in Lawton, Quanah viewed the remains in a casket, the baby in the arms of the mother; when assured that this was his mother, the great chief said, "Then I am satisfied. I have looked for her a long time." On December 10, 1910, the reburial took place in the Post Oak Mission Cemetery seven miles northwest of Cache and near the Star House.

Parker was then in his sixties and in failing health. After attending a medicine dance and peyote ceremony in late January 1911, he became very sick on the return train trip. Suffering from pneumonia, asthma and rheumatism, he was forced to bed on February 22, 1911, and turned to the tribal medicine man for relief. When Quanah died the next day, the medicine man flapped his hands over the body like the wings of a departing eagle. Cynthia Ann's boy died the richest Indian in the United States and the last Comanche chief; the federal government did not recognize a successor. Sadly, there were only 1,171 members of the Comanche tribe left in 1911 in contrast to the 1,597 Comanches at the Cache Creek

Agency in 1875. As a crowd of one thousand looked on, Quanah Parker was buried in the full regalia of a Comanche chief beside his beloved mother in the Post Oak Mission Cemetery.

Congress later appropriated money for a monument to him which was dedicated on May 30, 1930. The inscription was written by his daughter, Neda Parker Birdsong, and reads:

Resting here until the day breaks, and the Shadows fall, and darkness disappears, is
QUANAH PARKER
LAST CHIEF OF THE COMANCHES.
B   1852   D   FEBRUARY 23, 1911

The remains and markers of mother, daughter, and son were reburied in the Fort Sill Post Cemetery in 1957 because of the army's need for larger firing ranges around Fort Sill. The funeral oration was delivered by Major General Thomas E. de Shazo, who said:

... She is a shining example of motherhood in adversity everywhere ...
... We will foster the memory of his service and her devotion and valiant spirit that they both symbolize.

Quanah's Star House was moved into Cache, Oklahoma, at the same time. In 1960 his last surviving wife, Topay, donated his lance, warbonnet and other personal effects to the Panhandle–Plains Historical Museum at Canyon, Texas.

The Parker family has also been given lasting honors by the State of Texas. In 1936 the state authorized restoration architect Raiford Stripling to rebuild a log replica of Old Fort Parker. On May 1, 1941, Fort Parker State Park opened to the general public. The grave of Elder John Parker is located in the middle of the stockade by the flagpole. The towns of Quanah and Nocona and Parker County also bear witness to the family influence on Texas history. Each year since 1953 both Comanche and Anglo Parkers have met alternately in family reunions at Fort Parker and at Cache, Oklahoma.[3]

---

3. The 1983 reunion was featured in the October 1983 issue of *Texas Highways*. "Texas" Parkers came to this gathering from as far away as Washington, D.C. and California. Among the Oklahoma delegation were James Cox and Baldwin Parker, Jr., two of Quanah's grandsons. Cora Parker Shaw of Elkhart, Texas, brought four generations to the 1983 family reunion; her ninety-three-year-old cousin, Gaily Faith Parker Davis, also of Elkhart, was the oldest Parker present and both are descended from Cynthia Ann's uncle Daniel. To symbolize the peaceful coexistence of two cultures under one name, the Parkers of Texas presented a silver bowl to the Oklahoma Parkers, with the phrase "Yesterday, Today, Tomorrow" inscribed over a peace pipe.

Cynthia Ann Parker, mother of Quanah Parker, with her daughter, Prairie Flower.

Quanah Parker, last of the Comanche Chiefs
Courtesy Western History Collections,
University of Oklahoma Library

Quanah Parker in full "white man's" dress
Courtesy Western History Collections,University of Oklahoma Library

Quanah Parker, late in life
Courtesy Western History Collections, University of Oklahoma Library

Quanah Parker's home near Fort Sill, a large frame dwelling with outbuildings enclosed by a picket fence. Circa 1892.
Courtesy Smithsonian Institution National Anthropological Archives, Bureau of American Ethnology Collection

Quanah Parker in his home at Fort Sill, Oklahoma, near a portrait of his mother, Cynthia Ann Parker, holding her young daughter, Prairie Flower.

Courtesy Smithsonian Institution National Anthropological Archives, Bureau of American Ethnology Collection

Children of Quanah Parker, 1891–1893
Courtesy Smithsonian Institution National Anthropological
Archives, Bureau of American Ethnology Collection

Parker family portrait at annual reunion, Old Fort Parker,
1983. In the front are two of Quanah's grandsons, Baldwin
Parker Jr. and James Cox. Courtesy *Texas Highways* Magazine

Portrait taken at Carlisle, Pennsylvania, prior to a trip to Washington, D.C., where the group headed the Carlisle Indian students in the inaugural parade of Theodore Roosevelt. Shown are Little Plume, Blackfoot; Buckskin Charle, Ute; Geronimo, Apache; Quanah Parker, Comanche; Hollow Horn Bear, Dakota; and American Horse, Dakota, 1905.

Courtesy Smithsonian Institution National Anthropological Archives, Bureau of American Ethnology Collection

VI

L. H. McNelly:
The Ranger Who Kept On Coming

"You just can't lick a man who keeps on coming on."
This definition for courage came from a frail, soft-voiced
consumptive who spent half of his short life in the violent
service of Texas. Captain L. H. McNelly knew he was
dying when he took on the task of taming the Nueces
Strip. Brutal in his methods and impervious to pain, he
defied international law and the United States government to clean up a lawless situation. A border citizen
who knew many peace officers said of him: "McNelly was
always the ideal. He seems not to have had a single
weakness . . ." After his body was used up by the state, he
became a political scapegoat and was left helpless to fend
for his family. This is the story of a man whose iron will,
courage and daring set the standard by which future
Texas Rangers would be measured.

Leander H. McNelly, the son of P. J. and Mary Downey McNelly, was born in Brook County, Virginia, on
March 12, 1844. The small, thin, timid youth developed
consumption at an early age and enrolled in school to
train for the Methodist ministry. In the fall of 1860, the
family came to Texas hoping that the climate would im-
prove his health. The McNellys brought a herd of sheep

Texas Ranger Captain L. H. McNelly
Courtesy Western History Collections,
University of Oklahoma Library

John King Fisher
Courtesy Western History Collections,
University of Oklahoma Library

to western Washington County and started ranching with the young tubercular becoming a sheepherder. However, the Civil War was to turn this David into an unlikely Goliath.

Lee joined the Confederate army at age seventeen, enlisting at San Antonio on September 13, 1861, to serve in Company F, Fifth Regiment, Texas Mounted Volunteers. This unit was General Thomas Green's regiment of H. H. Sibley's brigade and Green made McNelly his aide after Val Verde during the New Mexico campaign. After fighting in the Battle of Galveston, Lee was ordered to Louisiana where on December 19, 1863, the nineteen-year-old soldier received a commission as captain of one hundred guerrilla scouts and later carried out a mission disguised as a woman. During the war his most spectacular achievement was the capture of Brashear City, Louisiana, and 800 federals with only forty men. To reach the city McNelly's men had to cross a long bridge. After darkness fell they marched back and forth across it for an hour, all the time shouting orders to unseen generals and colonels. At daybreak McNelly and his forty men rode into the federal camp under a truce flag and brazenly demanded unconditional surrender. After hearing the nighttime movements on the bridge, the Union officer assumed he was facing an army of thousands and gladly accepted the terms, allowing Lee to present General Green with 800 prisoners. McNelly was wounded in the Battle of Mansfield in April 1864, then spent the last months of the war leading a company of mounted scouts working out of Hempstead, Texas. His assignment was to round up deserters and his outfit was one of the last Confederate units to disband. It seems he also enjoyed a health reprieve, taking no sick leave or furlough in four years of fighting. McNelly then returned to farming west of Brenham, married, and had a girl and a boy.

However, his military talents did not go unrecognized. On July 1, 1870, Texas Republican Governor E.J.

105

Davis organized a State Police force to be headed by the adjutant general with McNelly as one of four captains. At first there were also eight lieutenants, twenty sergeants, and 125 privates with every local peace officer also serving as a member. This police force got off to an inauspicious start when the first director absconded with $34,000 in 1870. Citizens were soon accusing the hated State Police of killing prisoners allegedly trying to escape and of harassing voters; even some Radical Republicans thought them to be brutal and overbearing. Texas historian Walter Prescott Webb later described their career as "a story of official murder and legalized oppression."

McNelly's most controversial State Police assignment came with the declaring of martial law in Walker County. Trouble developed there after a Negro named Sam Jenkins told a grand jury he had been flogged, and was then murdered a few days later. Lee was sent to solve the crime and soon arrested four men. One was released after a courtroom hearing but the other three were ordered held over until the next term of the district court. The prisoners had been smuggled six-shooters and suddenly opened fire as McNelly was returning them to jail. They wounded Lee and Tom Keese before escaping and Governor Davis reacted to the jailbreak by declaring Walker County under martial law on February 15, 1871. The resulting military commission tried twenty men with one being given a five-year prison term. While recovering from his wounds, McNelly told a *Galveston News* reporter that the escape would not have occurred if the sheriff had searched the people entering the courtroom. He also expressed the view that martial law was unnecessary and told of his distaste for Governor Davis. When this police force that ex-Confederates referred to as "Texas traitors" was abolished on April 22, 1873, the editor of the *Dallas Herald* declared: "The people of Texas are today delivered from as infernal [an] engine of oppression as ever crushed any people beneath the heel of God's sunlight." Although McNelly stayed with the State Police until the bitter end, his popularity and reputation did not seem to suffer.

After the Texas Democratic party regained political control in 1873, Governor Richard Coke was confronted with an epidemic of lawlessness; in fact, a fugitive list or "Black Book" compiled by Adjutant General Steele contained over five thousand names and another five hundred feudists. To deal with the situation, the governor established two military forces: the Frontier Battalion was to fight the Indians in West Texas while a Special Ranger Force was ordered to suppress Mexican bandits and cow thieves in the Nueces Strip. McNelly was named captain of the Special Force which was financed from the beginning by rich stockmen along the Nueces River and from Goliad and Victoria counties.

Before going to southwest Texas, Captain McNelly was ordered to stop in DeWitt County and deal with an outbreak of the Sutton–Taylor feud. This so-called "bloody harvest" was set off in March 1874 after Bill Sutton was shot to death by Jim Taylor on the steamer *Clinton* at Indianola. Lee and a company of forty rangers arrived at Clinton, the DeWitt County seat, on August 1 to prevent a pitched battle between the two groups. A basic problem in handling the feud was getting witnesses into court alive and McNelly asked for reinforcements that autumn, describing both factions as ". . . turbulent, treacherous, and reckless." When Jim Taylor stood trial at Indianola on September 24, some 150 Suttonites announced plans to attend to see that he "got justice" so Lee's company was ordered there for the trial. Although there were no more major gunfights in the four months the rangers stayed in DeWitt County, McNelly never claimed to have accomplished much there. When he departed he blasted the laxity and inefficiency of local officers, claiming that the district attorney was drunk most of the time and "when sober is of no earthly account."

The spring of 1875 found Lee sickly and back on his cotton farm near Burton in Washington County. In April Governor Coke ordered him to organize a special force and proceed to Nueces County. It took him only two days to hire forty-one men for the Washington County Volunteer Militia, a group to become famous as McNelly's Rangers. Among the first to sign up was the youngest member, a powerfully-built teenager and recent arrival from Georgia named George (Josh) Durham. When he first saw his five feet, six inch, 135 pound leader, he described Lee as a "little runt of a feller" who looked like a "puny preacher." Many of these men were on the dodge and were wanted in other states. McNelly rejected most Texans, preferring daring youths born elsewhere who would not be shooting at their own relatives or friends. The majority came from the Old South and included Virginia farmers, Georgia woodsmen, Alabama blacksmiths, and Vermont scholars. Ranger Horace Rowe was a poet with a published book of verses while Rudd was from London, McKay came from Scotland, and McGovern was a native of Ireland. John B. Armstrong was named first sergeant and Dad Smith was the wagon boss, bringing his boy Berry along as a swamper.[1] Each man was to be paid thirty-three dollars a month and had to provide his own horse, saddle and sidearm. These men who rode out for Corpus Christi were to develop a fanatical loyalty to their leader and call themselves "Little McNellys."

On April 18, 1875, lawlessness in the strip between

1. Ranger Captain Armstrong's major claim to fame was his role in the capture of the killer gunman, John Wesley Hardin. Armstrong was one of four men who confronted the gunfighter in a smoker car at the Pensacola, Florida, railroad depot on August 23, 1877. However, it was two Florida lawmen who first grappled with Hardin and took his gun before Armstrong arrived from the other end of the train car and knocked him out. After bringing Hardin back to Texas to stand trial for killing Deputy Sheriff Charles Webb, Captain Armstrong shared the $4,000 reward with Detective Jack Duncan.

the Nueces River and the Rio Grande prompted the following telegram from Sheriff John McClure of Nueces County to Adjutant General William Steele:

Is Capt. McNelly coming? We are in trouble. Five ranches burned by disguised men near La Parra last week. Answer.

By this time ranchers in the Nueces Strip claimed to have lost 700,000 head of cattle to a network of Mexican rustlers and fences headed by Brigadier General Juan Cortina, Commander of the Line of the Bravo. As military chief of the Rio Grande frontier, Cortina used his diplomatic position to sign large contracts in Spanish Cuba for marketing stolen Texas cattle shipped from Mexico's Gulf port of Baghdad, the former Confederate cotton port near Matamoros. Cortina knew that international law prevented his raiders from being pursued across the Rio Grande so he brazenly stocked his own Caritas, Palito Blanco, Soldadito and Canela ranches with stolen Texas cattle. The raids even made him rich enough to buy his own ship for delivering Texas cattle to Cuba. After licensing these border bandit raids, some of them involving Mexican officers and soldiers, General Cortina took a percentage of the loot, charged a crossing fee on the Rio Grande, then paid two dollars per head for the stolen cattle. In 1872 he was indicted by a Brownsville grand jury as the "ranking cow and horse thief on both frontiers," but no lawman would dare attempt to bring Cortina to trial.

This was the situation facing McNelly's Rangers when they rode into Corpus Christi that spring of 1875. This sleepy settlement had become a center for counter-raiding by armed bands of local citizens (Minute Companies) who were hanging and killing innocent Mexicans in the area, burning their houses, and looting their ranches. When the rangers arrived the town was shuttered and expecting another bandit raid with no women or children in sight. McNelly was told of a March 26 raid on Nueces-town, some twelve miles away, that was led by Juan Cortina himself. Fifty heavily armed Mexicans had hanged one man, killed another, wounded two, and stripped and tortured a number of prisoners. Tom Noakes's store was also plundered and burned and his wife Martha was quirted on the back. After learning that the Mexican raiders had also taken eighteen brand-new Dick Heye silver-studded saddles, the ranger captain asked for a description of them, then issued the following orders to his men: "Empty those saddles on sight. Leave the men where you drop them and bring the saddles to camp." When Sol Lichtenstein, a prominent local storeowner, told him to pick out what supplies he needed and simply sign for them, Lee asked for thirty-six .50 caliber Sharps single-shot buffalo guns rather than repeating rifles. The Sharps weapon had a long range accuracy and McNelly, who "didn't want men who miss," expected his rangers to kill with the first shot.

After leaving Corpus Christi Lee let it be known that he would give a posse and all private armed bands only a few minutes to disband or else "consider them outlaws." He did, however, order his men to treat all law-abiding citizens with respect and not to raid gardens, enter homes unless invited, or shoot household dogs. Upon his arrival at Banquette, a town known as the "Sheriff's Deadline," McNelly was given copies of the "Black Book," which contained a listing of 228 pages of men wanted for crimes. In his search for these outlaws and Mexican raiders, the captain was to be a brutal, ruthless guerrilla warrior, making law as he went and dealing out justice on the spot. He arrested anyone who *might be* a suspect, then hoisted him by the neck a few feet off the ground to get information. McNelly would kill all prisoners on the spot if a rescue was attempted; in fact, his "jailer," Jesus Sandoval, made sure that no prisoner lived long.

"Casuse" Sandoval was a crazy, sadistic brute who

enjoyed torturing and killing Mexican bandits. He was the first Mexican to serve as a Texas Ranger after earlier owning a ranch above Brownsville. While he was away on a four-day trip, Mexican raiders burned his house, killed all his livestock and violated his wife and pretty fifteen-year-old daughter into such a state of shock that the two had to be confined in a Matamoros convent. To avenge his family Sandoval went on a long killing spree in Mexico, taking fifty victims before joining McNelly as a scout in 1875. There was a wild look about this graceful, daring rider with the long red hair and beard who so hated Mexicans. Since Lee did not have enough men to guard prisoners and could not risk turning bandits or spies loose, Casuse became his executioner, using either of two methods: Often his paint horse served as a trapdoor gallows to hang prisoners; at other times he would literally rip a head off by lashing a captive to a tree by the neck, looping his feet with a lariat tied to Sandoval's saddle, and slapping the paint horse's rump. The resulting death was described by ranger George Durham as being "too brutal" and making his "stomach to start turning flips."

When the rangers left Banquette, they had no tents and carried only a simple blanket and coffee pot. On their first patrol they moved out along the old Taylor Trail headed for Captain Richard King's Santa Gertrudis Ranch. At first sight it looked more like a fortress: two lookouts manned the tall steeple and the main ranch house contained an arsenal. When Captain King saw the "nags" they were riding, he remounted the entire company on splendid saddle horses with Captain McNelly picking out a five hundred dollar big bay named "Segal." During this brief stopover the "love bug" first bit young ranger Durham after he saw Mrs. King's niece, Caroline Chamberlain.

On June 5, 1875, scout Sandoval brought news that sixteen Mexican cattle raiders had crossed the Rio

Grande south of Brownsville headed for La Parra. A week later McNelly caught up with them at Palo Alto prairie near Laguna Madre. When the Mexican rustlers were spotted about 7:00 A.M., they bunched their stolen cattle on a small island in the middle of a salt marsh, then took a stand behind a five-foot bank on the opposite side. This lagoon was six hundred yards wide and eighteen inches deep, forcing the rangers to wade across in line. Before they charged Lee told his men, "This won't be a standoff. We'll either win completely or we'll lose completely. Shoot only at the target directly in front." He waited until he was within thirty paces of the Mexican position before opening fire; at this point the unnerved Mexicans broke for their horses and the battle became a series of hand-to-hand fights for six miles. When McNelly caught up with the bandit on the fastest horse, he was hiding in a Spanish dagger thicket. The two were only eight feet apart with the Mexican armed with a bowie knife and Lee having only one ball left. McNelly suddenly called out, "My pistol's empty. Bring me some shells." The outlaw then charged, grinning and saying, "Me gotta you now, me gotta you;" those were his last words as he died with Lee's last shot between his front teeth. George Durham claimed that a dying bandit asked for religious consolation, prompting McNelly to take a New Testament from his jacket pocket and conduct last rites. By the time the battle ended on toward noon, all twelve Mexicans driving the cattle were dead. The rangers had lost one man and and recovered nine new Dick Heye saddles and 265 head of cattle belonging to Richard King. McNelly had, in his words, "naturalized" the invading immigrants and put Juan Cortina on notice that the rangers had arrived in the Nueces Strip.

The body of sixteen-year-old Berry (Sonny) Smith, son of the ranger wagon boss, was tied on a horse and taken to McNelly's camp on the edge of Brownsville. After an elaborate funeral a hearse drawn by two fine black horses took his body to the town cemetery and Smith was buried with full military honors, including an escort of rangers and two companies of United States regulars from Fort Brown. In contrast, the bodies of the twelve Cortina raiders were stacked out in the open on the town plaza and left there to draw flies, guarded and unclaimed all day. McNelly ordered this done as a grisly example to show "how rangers deal with cow thieves." Five of the unburied corpses were citizens of Brownsville and it seems that Lee was also trying to bait a raid from across the river. When this did not occur, he turned the bodies over to Sheriff Browne the next day.

While his men camped near town, Captain McNelly ordered two front rooms in the Miller Hotel as his headquarters. After going hungry for days, it was a real treat to Ranger Durham to have a huge breakfast of flapjacks and side meat at Fort Brown. His leader was bothered by a bad cough and "looked peaked," staying in his room much of the time on a health diet of goat milk and meat. Although seemingly inactive, Lee was actually building up an effective spy system and getting daily reports. Policing the Nueces Strip with a tiny force of rangers required being in the right place at the right time; thus McNelly acquired spies among the bandits in Mexico whom he knew to be "tricky" and paid them regular salaries. He found these informers to be "reliable and trustworthy" and made the following frank admission: "I did not propose to interfere with their own individual stealing at all. I gave them liberty, when I was not in their neighborhood, to cross over with their friends, and get cattle and return again." The war chest to pay these spies came from members of the Stock Raisers Association of Western Texas and their president, Mifflin Kenedy. Richard King also supplied McNelly's Rangers with beef and sent them cash bonuses on at least two occasions.

From June until October of 1875, there were no major encounters and the captain was visited by his wife

Carrie and little boy "Rebel," who was paddled more than once when he played with ranger pistols. Although McNelly was "just plumb worn out," he did lead the twenty-nine men he had left on patrol and was tricked by scout Pete Marsele into waiting near the coast for four days with no grub while bandits spirited 800 head of cattle into Mexico some one hundred miles upriver. He was now facing complaints of Palo Alto being a "butcher job" and of his failure to turn in prisoners. Finally, after coming down with chills and fever in early October, McNelly turned command over to Lieutenant Robinson and took a furlough to his Washington County home. There Carrie put him to bed, nursed him, and rigged a cotton wagon as his camper when he returned to action later in the month.

McNelly's men followed a policy of terror during the months they camped near Brownsville. One of them, N.A. Jennings, later claimed that on nightly visits across the river to Matamoros, they were told to have fun and terrorize the Mexicans. In his words, their goal was to gain a reputation as "fire-eating, quarrelsome daredevils" by asserting themselves and trampling the "greasers." To this end, they often shot out lights and wrecked fandangos (dances) both across the river and in Brownsville. One Saturday night a particularly bold trooper named Boyd barged into a cantina alone, intent on breaking up the party. He began to shoot out the lamps but got off only three shots before the Mexican crowd pounced on him and knocked him senseless to the floor. Boyd would have been pounded to death if six other rangers had not come to his rescue, pistols in hand, and dragged him outside.

Since the rangers were patrolling near Fort Brown, the Mexican raiders started crossing their stolen herds a hundred miles up the Rio Grande at Las Cuevas and Camargo. Lieutenant Robinson reacted by moving the rangers to a camp at Rancho Las Rucias near Edinburg in October 1875. While awaiting orders from their sick leader, they went days without going on patrol. By mid-November Carrie McNelly had fed her husband back on his feet at Burton and he ordered his men to rush to Ringgold Barracks at Rio Grande City. The news was such a tonic to the restless men that they made a record ride, covering the sixty miles in five hours. Lee had learned that the Las Cuevas Ranch was to be the gathering point for 18,000 head of stolen Texas cattle. On November 12, 1875, he met with the Ringgold commander, Major A.J. Alexander, who promised that he would "instruct his men to follow raiders wherever I (McNelly) will go." Alexander's superior at Brownsville, Colonel Potter, also made the same commitment. The ranger captain thus assumed he had the support of the United States army if he dared to cross the river in pursuit of Mexican bandits. The stage was now set for the Las Cuevas War, the most heroic, violent and flagrant episode of these turbulent years.

On November 17, 1875, sixteen Mexican raiders took 250 head of stolen cattle across the Rio Grande at the Las Cuevas crossing. Shortly thereafter a detachment of U.S. Cavalry troops from Edinburg arrived there and set up camp on their side of the river. They were soon joined by Eighth Cavalry troopers from Ringgold Barracks, which was only ten miles away. After the senior officer present, Major Clendenin, took command of these one hundred troops and set up a battery of Gatling guns, Captain McNelly rode alone into the federal camp at noon the next day with a plan for a bold and illegal strike into Mexico. His objective, the Las Cuevas Ranch, was only three miles from the river crossing and was the headquarters of General Juan Flores, alcalde of the village and chief of the border cow thieves. Although Major Clendenin refused Lee's request for army troops, he did say that "if you are determined to cross, we will cover your return." McNelly then asked for volunteers to bring the cattle back and "learn them (the Mexicans) a Texas lesson." At that point all thirty members of his ranger company stepped forward.

At 1:00A.M. on November 19, McNelly's Rangers started across the Rio Grande three at a time in a leaky rowboat. They were all on the opposite bank by four o'clock but only five rangers had their horses. With guide Casuse Sandoval on the point, they started marching single file along a narrow cattle trail, surrounded by thick underbrush and dense fog. Their orders were to kill all except old men, women and children. At first dawn they reached a rail fence and Lee said, "Boys, I like your looks all right — you are the palest set of men I ever looked at. That is a sign you are going to do good fighting. In the Confederate army I noticed that just before battle all men get pale." The five men on horseback then let down the gate bars and led the charge; in the next few moments, the rangers killed nine Mexicans who were either on picket, chopping wood, or running from some sheds. During the melee a Mexican woman patting tortillas informed Lee that this was the Cachuttas, a line camp for the main Las Cuevas Ranch a half mile away. Old Casuse had led him to the wrong ranch! More importantly, McNelly had lost the advantage of a surprise attack.

The rangers hastily reassembled and took the left fork of the cow trail. When they reached Las Cuevas, they encountered some 250 Mexicans, one hundred of them mounted and led by Juan Flores. They also had artillery and were lined up between McNelly and the first ranch house. After exchanging shots for ten minutes, Lee ordered his men to break for the river in what became a series of brush fights. When they reached the Rio Grande, they formed a skirmish line using the riverbank as earthworks rather than trying to swim across. The pursuing Mexicans had assumed the rangers would try to swim the river so were caught completely off guard when Flores and a mounted force of twenty-five galloped to the top of the bank. Firing almost at point-blank range, McNelly's men killed the Mexican general in the first exchange of fire but most of his men scrambled into a nearby thicket.

While the rangers dug in along the riverbank and repulsed several attacks, Captain Randlett and forty U.S. soldiers of D Company, Eighth Cavalry, crossed the river into Mexico at 11:00 A.M.. In the meantime some two hundred soldiers arrived in the Mexican camp. At five o'clock that afternoon, a Mexican truce party appeared with a letter from the chief justice of the state of Tamaulipas, who was acting for the dead alcalde, Flores. He requested that McNelly withdraw his troops from Mexico and promised that the stolen cattle would be returned at Camargo the next day. Lee McNelly not only refused to recross until he had the stolen cattle and thieves in hand; he also had the audacity to promise the much superior Mexican force one hour's notice before he broke the truce and attacked. At sundown Randlett and his men were ordered back across the river by his superior, Major Alexander, leaving McNelly's Rangers alone in Mexico. During the night they dug a long trench between the bank and the water in anticipation of a desperate fight to the death.

On the morning of November 20, Colonel Potter wired Major Alexander from Fort Brown, giving him strict orders not to assist McNelly if he was attacked by Mexican forces on Mexican soil. Later on in the day, a messenger crossed the river with a telegram from United States Secretary of War Belknap, who advised Lee to return to Texas at once and reminded him that U.S. troops would not support him while in Mexico. McNelly wiped some stew out of his whiskers, chewed on his cigar, and then penciled the following reply on the back of the message: "I shall remain in Mexico with my rangers . . . give my compliments to the Secretary of War and tell him . . . to go to Hell." At three o'clock that afternoon, the American consul at Matamoros tried unsuccessfully to arrange Lee's surrender. At 4:00 P.M. Captain McNelly served notice that he would attack the Mexicans unless they met his earlier demands to return the cattle and thieves; a few moments later they agreed to deliver the stolen cattle at Rio Grande City at 10:00 A.M. on November 21. McNelly and his men then crossed back to Texas as darkness fell.

The next morning — a Sunday — the ranger captain took ten men up to Rio Grande City to receive the stolen cattle. At three o'clock that afternoon, twenty-five Mexicans finally showed up across the river at Camargo with only seventy-five head. McNelly and his "Death Squad," the name Durham gave the detail, went over by ferry and were told the cattle must be inspected before being delivered. Two members of the ranger detail later provided different versions of what happened next: George Durham claimed that McNelly took the customs captain hostage and threatened to kill him unless the cattle were delivered within the hour; Ranger Bill Callicott recalled that Lee gave the Mexicans five minutes to put the cattle across the river or else he would kill them all. Whatever the circumstances, the stolen cattle were promptly delivered on the Texas side of the river. After they were penned McNelly and his men went to Ringgold Barracks that night to get forage for their horses. During the visit a U.S. army captain became upset when a ranger private sat down by Lee. When informed that army privates were not allowed such a privilege with their officers, McNelly replied, "I wouldn't have a man in my company that I did not think was as good as I am."

On November 22 four young volunteers, including Durham and Callicott, were ordered to take the thirty-five stolen cattle carrying Richard King's "Running W" brand to his Santa Gertrudis Ranch. According to Bill Callicott, Captain King was amazed at McNelly's feat and remarked,

That was a daring trip. There is not another man in the world who could invade a foreign country with that number of men and all get back alive. Captain McNelly is the first man that ever got stolen cattle out of Mexico. Out of thousands of head I have had stolen, these are the only ones I ever got back, and I think more of them than of any five hundred head I have.

The famed rancher ordered his hands to saw off the right horn of each cow, then turn them out on the big range to graze in peace for life. He also proved to be a grateful and gracious host; Ranger Callicott said that

Captain King invited us to go up to the house, but we told him we were too dirty to go where there were ladies — we hadn't changed clothes in ten days. Then he told us to take our guns and pistols and go to a room over the warehouse. There we found plenty of nice clean blankets, pillows, chairs, table, wash bowl, towels, water, candles, matches — everything nice enough for a St. Louis drummer. We made our pallets and about dark our supper came — ham and eggs, butter, cakes, pies, in fact, everything good to eat with plenty of fresh buttermilk and coffee. Captain King's two daughters who had just graduated from school in Kentucky sent up two big pound-cakes tagged:
COMPLIMENTS OF THE TWO MISS KINGS TO THE MCNELLY RANGERS.

During the meal the lovely Caroline Chamberlain came in and asked for the bashful George Durham, who was hiding out behind a stove. When the ranger detail departed the next morning, Captain King provided all the grub they could eat on the hundred mile return trip.

In one sense, the Las Cuevas War was a ranger success. Border raids did drop dramatically as news of McNelly's raid spread through northern Mexico. A near-end to the border mini-wars came after Porfirio Diaz came to power in 1877, then assigned Juan Cortina to a meaningless ceremonial post in Mexico City where he was held under house arrest until his death. However, McNelly's

119

Las Cuevas raid was botched from the very beginning when Old Sandoval led the rangers to the wrong ranch, an error that saved the lives of the entire company. Expecting to be surrounded and cut off if he took Las Cuevas, Lee had hoped to create a situation that would oblige United States troops to cross the river in force and rescue him, something they had no intention of doing; in fact, he told army officers of his plans before crossing the river and admitted that the rangers could not get back alive without their aid. It should be recalled that Flores had artillery at Las Cuevas; if the rangers had surprised the Mexicans and captured the big house as planned, they would have been pounded to bits. McNelly later confessed his good fortune when he said, "I claim that to be the tightest place I was ever in for all to get out alive." It should also be noted that he failed in his original goal, getting back only part of the cattle and none of the thieves.

After the McNelly–Cortina border war, the Texas Rangers started the tradition of wearing star-shaped badges carved from Mexican ten-peso silver coins. By then Lee's hair and beard were sprinkled with gray and he had a slow, stooped walk, spending much of his time in Carrie's big camper wagon. In spite of failing health, he hoped that the pursuit of Devil's River cattle thieves would lead to a showdown with John Wesley Hardin's gang, pledging to rid the state of these "pests" for good if he met up with them. In April 1876, the grateful Captain King sent Lee's company thirty 44–40 Winchester repeating carbines; they were no doubt put to good use the next month when the rangers crossed into Mexico again in an unsuccessful attempt to recover stolen cattle.

In mid-May of 1876, McNelly's Rangers headed for Dimmit County and a showdown with King (John) Fisher. Lee had charged that all white citizens of the county were desperadoes and claimed that Dimmit County was "under a reign of terror from the men who in-fest the region." The ringleader of the rustlers, King Fisher, was a dashing, handsome dandy who allegedly killed twenty-six white Radical Republicans to avenge the killing of his father by Reconstruction police at Fort Worth. His headquarters on Pendencia Creek was ten miles northwest of present Carrizo Springs and he so dominated the region that a road branch sign read: "This is King Fisher's road. Take the other." On June 4 McNelly took twenty-five men but no warrants when he carried out a dawn raid on the Fisher ranch house, ordering his rangers to "give them the first shot." Surprisingly, the famed gunman and eight other wanted men were captured with no shots fired and Lee relieved the "King" of his two silver-plated, ivory-handled revolvers. These were the first prisoners that McNelly had ever taken alive! After warning Mrs. Sarah Vivian Fisher that they would all die if a rescue was attempted, he took the prisoners the thirty miles to Eagle Pass and turned them over to Chief Deputy Sheriff Vale of Maverick County.

Sheriff Vale first pointed out that Fisher's name wasn't in the Black Book nor was he under conviction or indictment. When he pressed McNelly for specific charges, the famed ranger retorted, "He's no stranger to you. He's a damn bandit and killer!" At this point, Fisher's lawyer replied, "That's an opinion, not a charge under Texas law." The attorney then demanded that Lee name the bandit victims and produce them as witnesses; he also insisted that McNelly produce the bodies of the homicide victims along with witnesses. When the lawyer proclaimed that he could not accept "the jungle law of some ranger captain," that was too much for young George Durham, who slapped him clear across the room before being sent outside by his leader. Fisher and his men were then released and given back their guns, prompting the sneering King to say, "Much obliged, captain," and McNelly to reply, "You've won, King. I'm licked." Lee then proceeded to lecture Fisher, warning him to get out of the outlaw business because he might not be so lucky next time.[2] To add insult to injury, McNelly's men also had to turn loose the 800 stolen cattle they had recovered.

The dispirited and exhausted McNelly was now coughing up blood and took to bed again at the Menger Hotel in San Antonio. After Lieutenant Robinson set up the ranger camp at Oakville west of Beeville, Lee ordered Durham and three others to come to him for duty. When the four entered the hotel sick room, George described his idol as "pretty puny" and being the "same color as the bed sheets." Between coughing spells McNelly ordered his men to clean up, get new clothes and haircuts, then browse around San Antonio to let folks see that they were just "human." It seems that McNelly had become a political embarrassment to Governor Coke, who was in election trouble because of the controversial way the rangers had carried out his orders. After a few days of such posturing, the four were sent back to Oakville where Lieutenant Lee Hall soon arrived to take temporary command of the Special Force.

In early October of 1876, Hall and twenty of McNelly's men were ordered to DeWitt County. Even though there had been 150 murders in the county, there had been no indictments and Judge H. Clay Pleasants was unable to hold court. When the rangers pitched camp near the courthouse in Clinton, it must have been a source of relief to the citizens. Hall and his men had come specifically to search for the murderers of Dr. Philip Brazell and his twelve-year-old son George. The well-liked Brazell, a church worker and school board member, had been dragged from his sickbed and killed the day before he was due to testify before the first grand jury called in

2. Fisher should have taken McNelly's advice. On March 11, 1884, he was ambushed and killed along with his drunken friend, Ben Thompson, in a gambling den over the Vaudeville Theater in San Antonio. Thompson had earlier given King some pants made of Bengal tiger skin, attire suited for the jaunty style of Fisher.

years. After Judge Pleasants ordered Hall to forcibly round up a grand jury and hold them in session, that body voted murder indictments against seven members of the Sutton clan, including Joe Sitterlee, deputy sheriff of DeWitt County, and Marshal Bill Meador of Cuero. When Lieutenant Hall was given warrants for their arrest, he resorted to tactics that McNelly would have approved.

After learning that Sitterlee was getting married on Christmas Eve of 1876 with the wedding party to follow at the bride's house, Hall and twelve rangers chose to attend as uninvited guests. When they arrived the marriage ceremony was over, the party had started, and the newlyweds had opened the dancing to the music of *Oh, Suzanna!* Lieutenant Hall suddenly burst through the front door shouting, "We're rangers. Joe Sitterlee, you're under arrest!" The room was full of Sutton clansmen, including all seven of those indicted for the Brazell murders. Although there were seventy men present, they had only sidearms while Hall's handful of rangers were armed with either Winchesters or double-barreled shotguns. With warrants in hand, Hall called out the name of each wanted man in a loud voice and all meekly surrendered. After the rangers collected all weapons, groom Sitterlee asked to continue the wedding dinner and dance until dawn. The sporting Hall agreed to the romantic request but took Marshal Meader hostage, warning that he would die if any rescue was attempted. For the next few hours, Hall's rangers went into the room two at a time to take part in the wedding festivities. At daybreak, however, the seven prisoners were taken to a ranger camp and remained in their custody on orders of Judge Pleasants. It is significant to note that Lee Hall later gave most of the credit for the success of his daring raid to his men and Captain McNelly.

The real showdown came when Judge Pleasants had to rule on applications for bail. Sensing the potential for bloodshed, he ordered a carriage sent to San Antonio to bring McNelly to the court hearing. On January 2, 1877, an armed crowd packed the DeWitt County courtroom with rangers lining the walls. The crowd grew silent when McNelly suddenly appeared at the judge's bench, service pistol in hand, and announced, "This court is now opening for regular business. Any man who lifts a hand to hamper its functions will die." Judge Pleasants then entered the courtroom and scathingly denounced the seven Suttonites as "midnight assassins, cowards and ambushers." He then eyed them and said, "When you deal with the Texas Rangers, you deal with men who are fearless in the discharge of their duty and will surely conquer you." Amid loud curses from the angry crowd, the judge then ordered Sitterlee and his cohorts held without bond in ranger custody. While four rangers stayed behind as the judge's bodyguards, Lee McNelly performed his last public service by escorting the seven to the Galveston County jail for safekeeping.[3]

When the Special Force was reorganized at Victoria on January 26, 1877, McNelly's name was dropped from the roll and Lee Hall was named as new captain. After complaining that McNelly's medical bill had accounted for one-third of the expenses of the entire company, Adjutant General Steele commended Hall for being "in the full vigor of early manhood and health." The public notice had McNelly resigning for reasons of health but the astute George Durham remarked that ". . . He was down to be fired. His kind of law-enforcing wasn't good politics." Lee had literally been used up by the state and was set adrift with no compensation. He retired to his Burton farm hoping "to get in some cotton" but never made a crop because he was too weak to work and too poor to hire

<hr>

3. The Sutton seven were taken to Austin in June 1877, then returned to Cuero. Their indictments were later thrown out because the rangers had forced the grand jury to return to work. Hence the seven were never convicted but their six years in jail served to break the spirit of the Sutton–Taylor feudists.

hands. He died of consumption at age thirty-three on September 4, 1877, leaving his beloved Carrie alone to raise a boy and girl. After Lee was buried in the family cemetery at Burton, his old friend and admirer, Captain Richard King, erected a splendid sixteen-foot-high red granite monument over his grave. In 1936 the state of Texas erected a monument in his memory in Cameron County. In 1967 a marker was belatedly placed in front of his grave by the Texas Historical Survey Committee.

Perhaps we should return to George Durham for a final tribute to Lee McNelly. After Texas Governor Richard B. Hubbard disbanded the Special Force, Durham returned to the Santa Gertrudis Ranch where Captain King hired him to do ranch police work. In 1882 George married his sweetheart, Caroline Chamberlain, and was named general foreman of the El Sauz Division of the King Ranch, a position he held until his death. Caroline Durham died in 1915 but her husband lived to be eighty-four, passing away on May 17, 1940. In his old age Durham dictated his memoirs, *Taming The Nueces Strip*; in the book the grizzled old ranger summed up McNelly's impact on his men with this poignant remark:

> And when I go, I'll go as a McNelly. I hope I overhaul him one more time. When I get Over Yonder, as I said, I want to go back to work for Captain if he's still running an outfit.

John Wesley Hardin at age twenty
Courtesy Archives and Special Collections
Southwest Texas State University

Photograph of John Wesley Hardin
after his fatal shooting
Courtesy Archives and Special Collections
Southwest Texas State University

VII

John Wesley Hardin: A Gunfighter and His Times

John Wesley Hardin was the greatest gunman in Western history and the most wanted, hunted and feared man in Texas. His autobiography lists forty shooting victims with names and places mentioned in great detail; he obviously kept some sort of tally, either from diary entries or newspaper clippings, but there is no sense of guilt, remorse or shame in his writing. It was his firm conviction that his victims brought their fate upon themselves, that all of his bloody acts were right, necessary and done on principle. He seems to have regarded some killings as a type of public service; after one such shooting over a gambling incident, Wes remarked that "the best people said I did a good thing." He was not a typical gunfighter: He killed only in self-defense; all of his victims except the first one were armed with either knife or gun; he was a loner who joined no gang; he never robbed or killed for pay; he never shot a man in the back. To the contrary, Hardin was a gentleman in appearance and manners, intelligent and polite, and a doting but absentee father who tried to instill high ideals in his children.

The Hardin family first came to Texas from Tennessee in 1825. James Gipson Hardin was justly proud of

127

both his father Benjamin, who served in the Texas Congress, and his uncle William B., a noted judge for whom Hardin County was named. At age twenty-two James became a licensed Methodist circuit minister and later taught school to supplement the family income. Preacher Hardin served Corsicana where he lodged in the home of Dr. William Dixon, who had a pretty daughter named Mary Elizabeth. The Dixons were a family of cultured, Southern aristocrats, a clan including three doctors and a rancher who were proud and quick to take offense. When James proposed to Mary Elizabeth, the Dixons gathered in the parlor and actually took a vote before accepting the struggling preacher into the family. John Wesley Hardin, the second of their five children and named after the founder of Methodism, was born at Bonham in Fannin County on May 26, 1853. Wes was to be his common name but his mother always called him Johnny. James Hardin was a strict father who taught his sons the importance of personal bravery and standing up for one's rights. It was his dream that Wes would become either a preacher, lawyer or teacher.

In 1855 the Hardins moved to Moscow in Polk County, just north of Livingston, where Wes grew into a handsome, personable and intelligent young man standing five feet ten inches tall and weighing 155 pounds. His father voted against secession but when the Civil War came, he recruited a company of volunteers although frail health caused by a childhood bout with whooping cough kept him at home. During the war Wes and his older brother Joe had such men's jobs as guarding their home and putting food on the table. By age nine Johnny was a fast draw and a deadly marksman who always aimed at the head when shooting effigies of President Lincoln. Toward the end of the war, the Hardins moved to nearby Sumpter where Wes was at the head of the class both in school and at playtime. At age twelve the chivalrous Johnny knifed a classmate who dared to in-

A younger Jane Bowen Hardin
Courtesy Archives and Special Collections
Southwest Texas State University

Jane Bowen Hardin in 1870s
Courtesy Archives and Special Collections
Southwest Texas State University

John Selman, 1878
Courtesy of The Denver Public Library,
Western History Department

sult a plump, cross-eyed girl. Soon after the war ended, the family learned that the wife, daughter and son of Mrs. Hardin's brother had been brutally murdered by Union soldiers in North Texas; by then Wes hated all men in blue uniforms.

On a November day in 1868, Wes went to visit his uncle, Barnett Hardin, to help out in harvesting the sugarcane crop. Against his mother's wishes the fifteen-year-old boy carried a pistol with him. At the time a muscular Negro man named Marge was working on the Hardin plantation. Marge was the former slave of Judge Clabe Houlshousen, the brother of Barnett's wife. During a break in the work, Wes and his cousin challenged Marge to wrestle and put him down twice. Wes scratched Marge's face the second time, bringing blood and causing the freedman to shout, "No white boy can draw blood from Marge and live!" After he threatened to get a gun and kill Wes, Uncle Barnett ordered him off the plantation. When Johnny started home the next day, Marge suddenly jumped into the road holding a heavy club, cursing and shouting that he intended to kill the white boy. Once Marge struck at him, Wes fired his pistol three times, leaving the Negro bleeding and moaning by the roadside; he died the next day at Judge Houlshousen's home. Describing his flight from this first killing in Polk County, Hardin later wrote:

> To be tried for killing a Negro meant certain death at the hands of a court backed by Northern bayonets ... Thus, unwillingly, I became a fugitive, not from justice, be it known, but from the injustice and misrule of the people who had subjugated the South.

Convinced that their son could not get a fair trial in a Reconstruction court, the Hardins sent Wes to stay with some friends named Morgan who lived twenty-five miles away at Logallis Prairie. After learning that three Union soldiers were looking for him, Wes went out to meet them. Hiding in a thicket along a dried-up creek bed, he first challenged the three riders, then killed them all with a shotgun and pistol after a "sharp fight" in which his arm was shattered. That night he returned to Sumpter to tell his scared, grief-stricken parents about the shootout. Surrendering him was now out of the question so Preacher Hardin took Wes to Navarro County to live with relatives near Corsicana where he was offered the job of teaching at a small school, and he finished out the three-month term. However, the lure of cowboy life and the nearby cattle trails caused Wes to reject the school offer for the next year. With his teaching salary he bought a black horse, fine saddle and became a cowboy. After trying his hand at gambling, he became an expert at poker, seven-up and betting on horse races. This new-comer with the darting eyes also gained a reputation as a "game kid" and fast-draw artist at shooting matches.

In the early spring of 1869 Wes and his cousin, Simp Dixon, killed two pursuing soldiers on Richland Creek near Corsicana. Mr. and Mrs. Hardin moved to Navarro County to better control him while brother Joe took Wes to Hill County and the trading town of Towash on the banks of the Brazos. When Joe returned to his parents, Wes stayed behind to gamble at the nearby Boles race track. On Christmas Day 1869 he won $500 in gold at the races. That night Hardin was invited to a game of straight draw by Jim Bradley of Hot Springs, Arkansas, a gambler with a killer's reputation. Since they were playing on a blanket on the floor, Wes took off his pistol and boots and proceeded to take Jim for a hundred dollars. The angry Bradley pulled a bowie knife, took all of Hardin's money, and chased him from the log house. While the Arkansas desperado was boasting in a Towash saloon, Wes returned with a borrowed six-shooter and killed him with a shot between the eyes.

Preacher Hardin then wrote his brother Bob, who had a farm near Brenham, and asked if his wayward son could live there as a farmhand. John Wesley started for this new life in late January 1870 but killed two more men on the way. While collecting some cattle wages at Horn Hill, he decided to take in the show at a one-ring circus. By pure accident he caused a roustabout to burn himself on the lip; the angry circus worker drew on him and was shot to death. At Kosse, Wes met a beautiful young lady who encouraged him to come calling. When the regular beau of his newfound girlfriend arrived on the scene and demanded money or his life, Wes had to kill him. Soon after he settled down on the farm, Texas was readmitted to the Union on March 20, 1870, and Union soldiers began to withdraw from the state. While on his frequent gaming trips into Brenham, Hardin's skills won him the nickname of "Little Seven-up" from the elegant gambler Phil Coe. Wes was in Brenham when he learned that the Reconstruction governor, E.J. Davis, had organized a state police force under his direct control. This force included 125 privates, one-third of them Negro, whose mission was to wipe out rebels and the Ku Klux Klan. They were empowered to police elections, take over towns or counties, and levy taxes to pay for martial law. When some of them were stationed in the Brenham area, Hardin told his uncle that it was time for him to move on.

In July 1870 Wes had a brief confrontation with the gunman Bill Longley at Evergreen. They met at the race track where Longley accused him of being a McNelly spy. When Hardin retorted, "That's a damn lie," and said he wouldn't be bullied, Bill apologized, then lost all his money to the younger gunfighter in a poker game. Wes then rode aimlessly for weeks before deciding to go home to his family. The Hardins were then living at Mount Calm on the line between Hill and Limestone counties. That summer the state police publicized a list of 2,870 fugitives and criminals with his name at the top and a reward of $800 for him dead or alive. At the time, brother Joe was in school studying law with Professor J.C. Landrum at Round Rock near Austin and the two suggested that Wes come there. Forced to go into hiding and study away from school at a secret creekside camp, he met with Joe to study books, lecture notes, and to argue points of law; Wes even slipped into Round Rock at night to take his final exams with Joe, and both graduated.

The young fugitive then headed for Louisiana in the fall of 1870 but was arrested at Longview as a suspect in a shooting. While in jail another prisoner sold him a smuggled .45 caliber pistol and Wes tied it under his left arm. In January 1871 a two-man state police escort started to take him back to Waco. When they made camp the second night and Captain John Stokes went to get corn for their horses, Hardin killed the single Mexican guard on watch and escaped to Mount Calm. His parents suggested that he go to Mexico but three state policemen captured him en route halfway between Waco and Belton; when a drunken guard fell asleep, he killed all three. Wes then stoped in Gonzales County to visit his four Clements cousins who were open-range cattlemen south of Smiley. One of them, Mannen, persuaded him to stay at his ranch on Elm Creek, help with the roundup, go on a trail drive to Abilene, and beat the law. As Jim Clements put it, "Why, every man who ever did a killing went up that way. No sheriff ever entered a cow camp hunting a man. Besides, Kansas officers pay no attention to Texas warrants because they couldn't collect a reward if they did jail a man." Thus persuaded Wes soon met sixteen-year-old Jane Bowen of Coon Hollow while attending a country dance. Jane was a dainty, shy, brown-eyed girl who loved to read and listen to the knowledgeable newcomer talk.

From the very beginning Wes Hardin was known by reputation in Gonzales County. It was apparent that this was no ordinary cowboy when he was appointed trail boss to take a herd of 1200 Longhorns up the Chisholm Trail. Even though he was the youngest hand in the outfit, he

133

drew a salary of $150, five times the pay of a regular drover. When his herd started north on March 1, 1871, there were 300,000 Longhorns on the trail in a line stretching almost a thousand miles across Texas. That spring the famed young gunman was the biggest news on the trail but the state police made no attempt to capture him. When the herd crossed the Red River into Indian Territory, trouble came on the South Canadian when Wes and the Clements boys refused to pay an Indian tax of ten cents a head for crossing the plains. Hardin killed two Indians when one threatened him with a bow and arrow and the other shot one of his steers. Before his herd reached Newton Prairie, Kansas, a Mexican herd just behind began to crowd him while the Mexican boss laughed at the complaining Wes as he would any other boy. The two first had a vicious fist fight in which Hardin lost a piece of lip and the Mexican suffered a broken jaw; then a prairie shoot-out ensued at full gallop in which Wes killed five vaqueros.

When the herd reached the North Cottonwood near Abilene, owner Columbus Carol went ahead to sell the cattle and "square" Wes with the new law there, Wild Bill Hickok, who had just become the "legal gunman" in the roughest, toughest town in the United States. "Squaring" the beardless, eighteen-year-old Hardin meant that Marshal Hickok would leave him alone unless he got way out of line. On June 1 Wes left the herd behind on the North Cottonwood and rode into Abilene to be paid. Marshal Hickok had a rule that no pistols could be worn in town but Hardin, thinking that being squared had made him an exception, openly strapped two pistols over an outfit of new clothes before he "made the town" the first night with Columbus Carol. The better-known marshal now faced a dilemma: To bluff or kill Wes would add little to his reputation; to shoot or jail him would bring trouble with the host of Texans in town. Wild Bill arranged a meeting where the two had a few drinks and a long talk during which he called his potential adversary "Little Arkansas" and ignored the pistols. Hickok decided to avoid the young gunman as much as possible but was forced to take action two days later when he walked into a noisy saloon, saw Hardin, and said, "Young man, you'd better get rid of your guns till you're ready to leave town." When Wes flatly refused, the two stepped out into the street; in a flash Hickok got the drop on him and said he was under arrest. Hardin pulled his pistols from the holster with muzzles turned inward and offered them to the marshal; then with lightning speed he suddenly reversed the pistol positions and had the drop on Hickok! This old trick — the "border roll" — had evened the score so the two had a drink and declared an uneasy truce. According to Wes, Bill said, "You are the gamest and quickest boy I ever saw. Let us compromise this matter and I will be your friend." On that very night, however, Hardin killed one of Hickok's men, a drunk in a cafe who had cursed Texans and wounded a Texas cowpuncher named Pain. Wes then quickly left Abilene and hightailed it to the North Cottonwood camp thirty-five miles away.

When he arrived there he learned that a friend, Bill Coran, had been shot in the back by Juan Bideno, a Mexican boss herder who had been fired for loafing. Bideno had escaped and headed for Texas, so some of the cattlemen offered to pay his expenses if Wes would track him down; he accepted when they agreed to go to Abilene, get a warrant, and have him deputized. After leaving camp on June 27, 1871, Hardin caught up with the Mexican badman south of Wichita at a town on Bluff Creek. Bideno was eating in the back room of a saloon when Wes asked him to surrender; Juan instead drew a pistol with his left hand from under the table and died with his face in his food and a bullet between his eyes. The cowboys celebrated at Abilene on June 30 by starting a pot for Hardin in a gambling hall; he received $1,500 in gold in less than an hour which only added to his prestige. On July 3 Marshal Hickok locked up his cousin, Mannen Clements, for killing two Gonzales men on the trail. After four hours of carousing together, Wes persuaded Wild Bill to let him have the jail keys and Mannen was a free man by midnight. On the night of July 7, Wes was awakened by a noise in his American Hotel room. After killing a hired assassin holding a knife, Hardin heard Hickok shouting orders on the stairs, then jumped out a window to the safety of a balcony and made good his escape wearing only a shirt and drawers. A posse of three chased him back to the cow camp where Wes got the drop on them and sent his pursuers back to Abilene unarmed and undressed!

The young gunman killed ten men on this trail drive, making a total of twenty-three victims before his eighteenth birthday. Homesick to see Jane Bowen, he hurried back to Sandies country to find that the state police force had been doubled in size with their main patrols being in Gonzales and DeWitt counties. In September 1871 he visited the bar at Pilgrim's place and learned that two Negro state policemen had been looking for him. One of them, Green Paramoor, came in and proclaimed, "Ah's got you-all, bad white boy!" Wes first laughed and finished his drink, then started to give Paramoor both pistols, butts forward; in an instant he rolled them and killed the trooper. Rushing outside he shot John Lackey off his mule; the wounded policeman lost some teeth and was left with an underbit lip but managed to escape by diving into a nearby lake to hide. When this news reached Austin, Governor Davis sent a posse of fourteen Negroes to get Hardin, dead or alive. The lone gunman chose to take the offensive and charged the entire posse north of Salty Creek, putting bullets in the heads of three before the survivors scattered "sadder and wiser," according to Wes.

After considering a move to Big Bend country to

start anew, Hardin decided to stay in Gonzales County and married Jane Bowen in March 1872. They moved into a three-room house on Fred Duderstadt's ranch in the Sandies and Wes turned to buying horses in the country around Corpus Christi to sell in Louisiana. On one such return trip that August, he stopped to roll tenpins in John Gates's saloon at Trinity City. After he beat a local young bravo, Phil Sublet, six straight games, the two began to argue and Wes slapped Phil in the face. The sore loser returned later with a shotgun and blasted Hardin in the left side with many of the buckshot lodging in his intestines and back. In agonized pain he was carried to a Dr. Carrington who spent an hour probing for and removing half a dozen pellets; even though no opiates were used during the operation, the patient made no sound. Wes was first placed in a local hotel room for a week and ordered to remain quiet if he hoped to live. To escape the state police, he was forced to move twice, first in a cot on a springless wagon and then on horseback. By the time he reached the Harrell ranch in Angelina County, his stomach pains were so fierce that Wes decided he had only one hope of living: he would surrender to an acquaintance, Dick Reagin, the sheriff at Rusk. On September 4, 1872, Sheriff Reagin arrested Hardin at the Watson ranch, agreed to give him medical care, pay him one-half of the reward money, and take him to Austin. While convalescing in a local hotel, Wes was sent food by admiring ladies. Within three weeks he was able to travel and in early October was transferred to Gonzales to stand trial for killing the Negro state policeman at Pilgrim's. On October 10, Sheriff W. E. Jones said that "his friends would be in to see him" and Mannen Clements smuggled Hardin a hacksaw file to cut the jail bars. With guards on duty telling him when to work, he completed the job that day and was pulled through the stubs of the cut bars by a horse. However, the tight squeeze ripped off his shirt and left him with deep back, chest and hip cuts.

At this time Gonzales, Wilson and DeWitt counties were living under a threat of violence because of the Sutton–Taylor Feud. This war was triggered in March 1868 at Bastrop when Deputy William Sutton killed cousins Charlie and Buck Taylor; the first victim was accused of stealing cattle and Buck died when he sought revenge. The sons of Creek Taylor then became rebels much as Wes Hardin and began to best Union soldiers in the area while Jack Helm, a captain in the state police, organized some fifty gunmen into the "Regulators" to fight the Taylors. When William Sutton joined him the group became known as the Sutton Party. Even after both quit the state police and Helm became sheriff of DeWitt County, the two continued to head the band. Although the Clements family and Wes took no active part in the feud, they did sympathize with Jim and Bill Taylor, cousins of the two slain men.

On February 6, 1873, Wes and Jane's first child, Molly, was born at Gonzales. A few days later Pitkin Taylor, the leader of the Taylor clan, died of wounds suffered in a recent ambush. At his funeral Bill Sutton stood in full view on the other side of the Guadalupe River; his laughing, cursing and shooting prompted the grieving eldest son, Jim Taylor, to swear that he would wash his hands in Sutton's blood! Both sides then redoubled their efforts to recruit Wes Hardin. On April 9, 1873, Wes and Sheriff Helm met on the trail between Gonzales and Cuero. Hardin dared the sheriff to arrest him, then rejected an offer of friendship and Helm's request that he join the Sutton party. While the gunman was in Cuero shipping horses the next day, he encountered Helm's chief deputy, J.B. Morgan, in a saloon. The drunk Morgan announced that he intended to arrest Wes, who stepped outside and was forced to kill Morgan after he drew his pistol. It was this killing that put Hardin with the Taylor faction.

There was rejoicing throughout Texas when the

state legislature, over the veto of Governor Davis, dissolved the state police on April 22, 1873. Many Texans believed that it was Wes Hardin who had vanquished this despised organization from the state. On April 23 he returned from the range to find Jane crying; it seems that Jack Helm and a large group had surrounded their house, then threatened and insulted her. To Wes, who never spoke a profane word to a woman, this incident justified killing on sight. When their families suffered the same indignity, Mannen Clements and George Tenelle also joined the Taylor party. In May, Hardin and Jim Taylor met Sheriff Helm at the small cattle center in Wilson County to discuss some sort of truce. While Jim was having a drink in the saloon, however, Helm slipped up behind him, put a pistol in his back, and said he was under arrest. Seeing this betrayal from the saloon door, Wes shouted, "Don't move!" The sheriff then made a fatal mistake: he turned his pistol slightly toward the door and died instantly. After the slaying Hardin said:

> The news soon spread that I had killed Jack Helm, and I received many letters of thanks from the widows of the men whom he had cruelly put to death. Many of the best citizens of Gonzales and DeWitt counties patted me on the back and told me that was the best act of my life.

In November 1873, E.J. Davis was defeated in the gubernatorial race by Democrat Richard Coke. The following March Wes, the Clements brothers, and the Taylors were branding cattle on the San Marcos for a second drive to Kansas when they received word that Bill Sutton and Gabe Slaughter were driving a herd to Indianola. Joe Hardin was visiting his brother at the time so he and Alex Barrickman checked into Smith's boardinghouse at Indianola for a couple of days to spy on the two. When they learned the date that Sutton was going to load his cattle in the hold of the steamer *Clinton* and start a vacation trip to New Orleans, the spies sent word to Jim and Billy Taylor who rode for Indianola seeking revenge. On March 11, 1874, the Taylors boarded the *Clinton* and made for the dining room on the upper deck where Bill Sutton and his wife were eating. In an instant the acrid smell of gunfire replaced the tantalizing scent of fine food. Jim Taylor killed Sutton as his horrified wife looked on; Billy Taylor gunned down Slaughter, whose body fell on top of his partner. It was this blood vengeance of the Taylors that caused the state to reorganize the Texas Rangers with the Frontier Battalion being assigned first to DeWitt and Gonzales counties. With the "heat" on again, Jim Taylor and Hardin decided that this would be an opportune time to take another herd to Abilene.

Wes and his family went ahead to visit his brother and parents at Comanche, 130 miles north of Austin, where Joe Hardin was a lawyer, realtor and postmaster. On May 26, 1874, Wes and his cousins, Bill Dixon and Jim Taylor, went to a horse race at Comanche where he won $3,000 and heard that Charles Webb, a deputy sheriff from nearby Brown County, had boasted at the track that he intended to kill Hardin. The two later met in front of the Polk Wright Saloon where Wes asked if Webb was there to arrest him; Charles said no, that he had no warrant. As the two walked into the saloon, Webb suddenly drew his gun and fired into Hardin's side. The wounded gunman whipped out a concealed pistol and shot Charles, who fell to the ground dead with a bullet in his head. It is ironic that the one killing that would send Wes to prison occurred on the night of his twenty-first birthday. This was clearly a matter of killing in self defense so Hardin surrendered to Sheriff Dave Karnes. After an angry lynch mob gathered outside the jail, Karnes gave Hardin and Jim Taylor their guns and let them escape and make a run for it with 150 vengeful residents of Brown County in hot pursuit.

After stopping at the Hardin home, the two went

into hiding at Round Mountain four miles away, then started for Gonzales County and arrived near Austin on June 5. Two days later they received news that Joe Hardin had been arrested by the Rangers and sheriff for his own protection and placed in the Comanche courthouse. Around midnight on June 5, a mob had stormed the building, hanged Joe and his cousins, Tom and Bud Dixon, on the square, and then divided the Hardin–Taylor herd. This sad and explosive situation caused his father to send word to Johnny to stay away or else the whole family would be killed.

Wes Hardin was now sure that "mob law" was supreme in Texas and that he must leave the state. After a brief return to the Sandies, he went to his uncle's home at Brenham where his oldest cousin, Harry Swain, the town marshal, volunteered to go to Comanche and get Jane and year-old Molly. The three of them then went into hiding at New Orleans awaiting the arrival of Wes by horseback. After taking the name of John H. Swain, the fugitive took his family to Cedar Keys, Florida, by steamboat in June 1874. The Swains first settled in Gainesville, Florida, where Wes briefly operated a saloon and grocery store. After subscribing to the *Galveston News* to keep up with Texas developments, he learned that the state legislature had offered a reward of $4,000 for his capture. Hardin quickly resettled in Micanopy, then moved to Jacksonville where he butchered and shipped cattle for a year. After John Wesley, Jr., was born on August 3, 1875, his father began to be shadowed by what he thought were two Pinkerton detectives; they were actually Texas Rangers. Wes sent his family to live with Jane's Alabama relatives, then he and a friend named Gus Kennedy killed the two sleuths at a depot on the Florida–Georgia line. In early 1877 Mr. Swain settled just north of the Florida line at Pollard, Alabama, where he bought and sold horses and entered into a logging partnership.

In late 1876, Texas Ranger Captain John B. Armstrong was assigned to the Hardin case and moved to Cuero. His partner was detective Jack Duncan of Dallas, who was appointed a special officer by Governor R.B. Hubbard in the spring of 1877 and given the specific assignment of tracking down Hardin. Duncan took the name of Mr. Williams, moved to Gonzales County disguised as a laborer needing work, and soon became a friend of Neal Bowen, Jane Hardin's father. A break in the case finally came when Brown Bowen wrote a letter to his father Neal telling of Jane's baby daughter Callie, who was born on July 15, 1877; in the letter Brown remarked, "My sister joins in sending love." Duncan managed to intercept and read the letter which was sent from Pollard, Alabama. To further secure his "cover," Duncan arranged for Armstrong to "arrest" him at Gonzales, take him to Comanche, and identify him as one of the Hardin gang. The detective then traveled to Pollard as a transient, learned for himself the true identity of John H. Swain, and wired Armstrong to come and help capture Hardin.

John Armstrong left Austin on August 18, 1877, with orders from Adjutant General William Steele to arrest Hardin. When he arrived at Montgomery, Alabama, two days later, he learned that Wes was in Pensacola, Florida, on a gambling trip. On that very day Hardin's true identity had also become known in Florida by William Dudley Chipley, the general manager of the Pensacola Railroad. As the *Atlanta Constitution* later reported it, a drunk Hardin had attempted to shoot a Negro at a train station-hotel. When Mr. Chipley refused to stop the fleeing black man, Wes stuck a pistol in his face; a fight ensued in which Chipley took the weapon and struck Hardin over the head with it. After the humiliated gunman threatened to kill him, Chipley offered to help Armstrong and Duncan with their plans in order to ". . . rid the country of such a scoundrel."

It was decided to attempt the arrest of Hardin fifty

miles to the south at Pensacola rather than at his home in Pollard where relatives and friends were likely to help him. Chipley even provided the two Texans with a special train car and the three arrived at Pensacola on August 22. After scouting around town Duncan located Hardin in a poker game and learned that he was taking the 5:00 P.M. train home the next day. At this point the pursuers sought the help of William Henry Hutchinson, the sheriff of Escambia County, who volunteered to arrest Wes on the street. The others vetoed that offer as being too risky and decided instead to make their move once Hardin was on board the train and in an isolated position. It was further agreed that Hutchinson and his deputy, A.J. Perdue, would receive $500 for their help in capturing the gunman.

On the afternoon of August 23, 1877, the train car was spotted parallel to the ornate Pensacola depot where twenty deputized men were hidden inside. Only five men — Hutchinson, Perdue, Armstrong, Duncan and Chipley — were to attack Hardin on board; they would enter the car simultaneously from both ends just as the train prepared to pull out. Wes was seated in the rear of the smoker car, facing the front end; with him were Jim Mann, Shep Hardie and Neal Campbell. All four had shotguns in the baggage rack above their heads but only Hardin and Mann carried concealed handguns. The group had just started a card game when Wes stopped to make small talk with Hutchinson and Perdue as they strolled through the car. Shortly thereafter the two Florida lawmen reentered the car from the rear; Hutchinson brushed by Hardin, wheeled and said, "I believe I want you." Although caught completely off guard, Wes exclaimed, "Damn you, take that!" and viciously kicked the sheriff in the groin with both heels. Hutchinson then struck Hardin across the face with a pistol before he and Perdue jumped on the gunman. As the three were grappling, Hutchinson grabbed the .44 cap and ball pistol suspended between Hardin's shirt and undershirt and yanked it out with such force that he ripped the shirt off; a second more and Wes would have had his pistol out. Only after the sheriff tossed the feared gun aside did Armstrong and Chipley arrive from the opposite end of the car; the four quickly overpowered Hardin and Armstrong knocked him out. After he was finally bound, Wes told Sheriff Hutchinson, "I have killed twenty-seven men, and if I could have got my pistol out you would have made it twenty-eight."

During the melee twenty shots were fired from both in and outside the train car. Nineteen-year-old Jim Mann fired at Armstrong, then was shot as he tried to escape by jumping out the car window, and died outside on the depot platform. It is likely that this innocent young man assumed that his party was being attacked by robbers. There is another irony in the capture of John Wesley Hardin: the two Florida lawmen who actually risked death in the fracas were ignored in the standard historical accounts while Ranger Armstrong received most of the credit.

Prisoner Hardin was released to the custody of Armstrong and Duncan at the Florida line. He was taken by train from Pollard to Montgomery where on August 24 he was formally charged with the murder of Deputy Sheriff Charles Webb. That same day J.W. Watts made an unsuccessful attempt to have Hardin released on a writ of habeas corpus. En route to Texas Wes sent his first letter to his wife and three children at Whiting, Alabama, telling Jane that Brown Bowen's letter was the cause of his arrest. Trying to comfort and reassure her, he said in part:

> ... Jane they Had me foul yes very foul I was Sitting in the Smoking Car ... with my arms Stratched on the Side when they came in. 4 men grab[b]ed me one by each arm and one by each Leg so the[y] Strached [stretched] me locking and quick ... Jane I am in good Hands now they treat me Better than you have any

Idea and assure me that I will not be mobed and that when I get there that the Governor will Protect me from a mob and that I will have the Law. Jane Be in cheer and dont take trouble to Heart But look to the Bright Side Jane I have not murded any Body Nor rob[b]ed any one But what I have done in Texas was to Save my Life Jane time will Bring me out . . .

There were large crowds along the train route and Wes continued to fear death at the hands of a mob. A Mr. Roe traveled from Memphis to Texarkana just to see Hardin and said, "Why, there is nothing bad in your face. Your life has been misrepresented to me. Here is $10. Take it from a sympathizer." There was a throng awaiting the train at the Palestine, Texas, depot and one of them shouted, "What have you got there?" Wes replied, ". . . a panther."

Hardin's train arrived at Austin on August 28 and he was assigned a lower cell near the entrance in the new Travis County jail. Among the seventy to eighty other prisoners there was Brown Bowen, who was arrested in Alabama on September first. Wes was allowed numerous interviews with reporters who described him as being pleasant and handsome, having a compact build, and wearing a modest mustache and whiskers in the French style. Some female admirers even sent cakes and roses to this killer gunman. When Hardin was taken to Comanche a month later to stand trial for killing Charles Webb, he was carrying thirty pounds of chain and escorted by a sheriff, five deputies, and twenty Rangers. At the trial there were no witnesses to testify in his behalf and it took the jury only a few hours to find Wes guilty of second degree murder and set his sentence at twenty-five years in prison. When the escort party camped at Brushy Creek on the way back to Austin, a fortuneteller made the uncanny prediction that Hardin would be attacked from the rear and killed if he was not careful.

A family crisis developed while Wes was still at Austin. Jane's brother Brown was arrested at Pollard and brought back to Texas to face murder charges; six years earlier he had shot Tom Halderman in the back at the Billings store at Smiley. Bowen was taken to Gonzales County for trial where he was convicted and sentenced to die by public hanging. In appealing to the Court of Criminal Appeals for a rehearing of his case, Brown claimed that Wes Hardin had killed Halderman. Jane's father Neal asked his son-in-law to take the blame since he was liked in Gonzales County and could "come clean there." Wes said he had no choice but to refuse and callously rejected another final plea for a statement that would save Brown's life. Brown Bowen went to the gallows on May 17, 1878, as a crowd of 4,000 looked on. On May 29, only days after Bowen's execution, Mannen Clements wrote Hardin to tell him that Neal Bowen had come to Gonzales with two rolls of greenbacks, $500 in all; the local talk was that Jack Duncan had given Neal the money as part of the reward for capturing Wes! The embittered father also went before the Cuero grand jury and revived the 1873 Morgan killing with Wes indicted for murder as a result. Jane took her husband's side during this ordeal, turning her back on her own family.

After the Texas high court affirmed the sentence of Wes Hardin because of the enormity of his crimes, he entered the state penitentiary at Huntsville on October 5, 1878. At first the surly, defiant convict Number 7109 thought only of breaking out of Rusk Prison. His first of numerous escape attempts was an elaborate plan to actually take over the prison. There were four small buildings in the prison yard with the wheelwright's shop at one end and the armory at the other. The conspiracy involved using eighty long-termers to excavate from the shop to the armory, then free all the inmates except the rapists. Working in short shifts with one man at a time digging with a spoon, they tunneled to the armory floor in a month. However, spies informed the superintendent of the scheme the very night that Hardin's cohorts were going to cut through the floor. After all suspects were arrested, Wes was first placed in solitary confinement for fifteen days. In January 1879 he received the limit of thirty-nine lashes with a whip because of his mutinous conduct; he later wrote that "my sides and back were beaten into a jelly . . ." On January 9, 1880, Hardin got another twenty lashes for conspiring to escape by bribing a guard. Entries in the prison records reveal that he was punished ten other times for such offenses as throwing food on the floor, laziness, inattention to work, and gambling.

In the fall of 1883 an abscess from his old Sublet wounds left Wes deathly ill and bedridden for a year. At this point an old friend from Chisholm Trail days came to his rescue. Ben McCulloch, a prison official and former Ranger captain, arranged for Hardin to have light tasks in the tailor shop during his recovery. It was also McCulloch who gave the rebellious convict some much-needed guidance. Ben told Wes that he could cut ten years off his prison term with good behavior and suggested that he take advantage of his educational opportunities while behind bars. Realizing that he would be only forty-one years old if he could get out in fifteen years, the chastened gunman promised McCulloch that he would make good in prison.

Wes Hardin became a model prisoner, reading and studying the rest of the day after finishing his work in the shoe shop. After reading the entire *Bible* and theological books, he turned to the works of Shakespeare and the dictionary while developing an extensive vocabulary. He became superintendent of the Sunday School, headed the debate team, and started studying law in 1889; in fact he was allowed to leave prison to take the bar exam and his family claims that he scored highest in a group of seventy candidates. Wes also began to send numerous letters of instruction and admonition to his children. Writing to John Jr., on July 3, 1887, he said:

> . . . I wish to speak to you of principles which if you observe and cling to them will be of far more value . . . Truth, my son, is a rare and precious gem . . . Justice is a gem rich & rare a full brother to truth . . . Now my son there is but one way to protect the character, protect wealth, your possessions, & that is by a strict adherence to truth & justice.

However, there must have been some behavior lapses: the Rusk prison records show that on May 26, 1893, Wes received twenty lashes for impudence and trying to incite convicts to riot.

While her husband was involved in a self-improvement program, Jame Hardin eventually returned to the Duderstadt ranch and began to work herself to death running a farm. She still considered Wes the head of the house and required the three children to write him requesting permission for various activities. It seems that their father thought he had an uncontrollable criminal mind; fearing that the trait would be inherited by his offspring and that they might follow in his footsteps, he pleaded with Jane to raise the children to be like her.

In 1891 Wes found an ingenious way to see his family. His scheme involved standing trial for the old 1873 Cuero murder indictment, pleading guilty to the charge of manslaughter, and hoping that a two-year minimum sentence could run concurrently with his present term. District Attorney Davidson was agreeable to the idea simply to get the old case off the docket so Hardin's trial started at Cuero on January 1, 1892, where Fred Duderstadt brought Jane and the children to visit him in his cell. The still robust, youthful-looking Johnny must have been shocked by his wife's appearance: she was frail and stooped with hollow cheeks and gray hair. However, her tired face glowed with pride when Wes presented an eloquent plea in court for a minimum sentence that would run concurrently with the rest of his long term. It took the jury only five minutes to find him guilty of manslaughter and to make such a recommendation.

Hardin went back to prison to work on a written petition for a full pardon that would restore his civil rights at the end of his term. After his Cuero trial a flood of petitions calling for his freedom were sent to Austin; these appeals came from Travis, Gonzales, DeWitt, Trinity, Polk and Ellis counties. Shortly after Wes received a letter stating that Jane was critically ill, she died at age thirty-six on November 6, 1892, and was buried in Asher Cemetery near Old Davy and the Mound Creek settlement. The children went to live with Fred Duderstadt while her distraught husband was in a daze for weeks. It must have seemed a rather empty victory when Wes was released from prison on February 17, 1894, after serving sixteen years and five months. After a reunion with his children at the Duderstadt ranch, he went to the Asher Cemetery, looked down on Jane's unmarked grave, and remarked, "About everything good I ever hoped for is buried here."

On March 16, 1894, Hardin received a full pardon for both convictions from Governor Jim Hogg, restoring his full citizenship and right of suffrage. Two weeks later he moved his family to Gonzales where he obtained a license to practice law and opened an office in the Peck and Fly Building on the courthouse square. Although the reformed gunman neither gambled nor drank and attended the Methodist church each Sunday, he had few clients and the girls soon went back to the Duderstadt ranch, leaving only John Wesley, Jr., with his father. Wes's dream of a new life began to fade when he unwisely jumped into local politics. In 1894 there was a heated race for sheriff of Gonzales County with W.E. Jones the Democratic nominee and Deputy Sheriff Bob Coleman the Populist candidate. Hardin became the key issue in the campaign after he wrote a newspaper article in the *Drag Net* claiming that the corrupt Jones in 1872 had allowed him to escape the Gonzales jail, had protected him from arrest, and was thus unfit to be a law officer. Wes even made his office Coleman's campaign headquarters and the war of words became so heated that John Wesley, Jr., was taken back to the Duderstadt ranch for his own safety. Hardin announced that he would leave town if Coleman was defeated and when Jones won the November election by only six votes, he kept his word. While packing his bags he was inspired to write the story of his life after finding a large stack of old letters that Jane had saved for him.

After telling the children goodby at the Duderstadt ranch, he moved to Junction on the advice of his brother, Jeff Davis, and opened a law office. At Christmastime he met Miss Callie Lewis, the teenage daughter of a prominent rancher, and the two impulsively married on January 8, 1895. When a county-wide ball was held in their honor and the couple did not appear, Captain Lewis went to see them and found his daughter crying; it seems that Jeff Davis Hardin had joked about her tender years. Callie asked her father to take her home and demanded that her husband leave and not return. The humiliated Hardin quickly moved to Kerrville to write his book and never saw his "wife" again.

In the spring of 1895, gunfighter James "Killin' Jim" Miller of Pecos asked Wes for legal help. Miller's wife was a daughter of Mannen Clements, a favorite cousin of Hardin. Miller was involved in a feud with ex-sheriff G. A. "Bud" Frazer and was suing him for assault with intent to murder. Hardin agreed to help, the case was moved to El Paso on a change of venue, and he arrived there on April 1, 1895. After the Frazer trial ended in a hung jury, Wes rented an office in the First National Bank building and tried, with small success, to establish a law practice. The town certainly did not lack for potential clients: El Paso was full of killers and robbers and offered them a sanctuary because of its proximity to Juarez, Mexico. The reformed gunfighter was used to hero worship and immediately began to make the rounds of the saloons and gambling halls where his name aroused instant fear and respect. On May 1 and May 2, 1895, he brazenly walked away with the pot after losing at poker and craps in two El Paso saloons. Since he had little law work, Hardin spent most of his time drinking, gambling, and writing his autobiography.

Wes roomed at the boardinghouse of Annie Williams as did Mrs. Helen Beulah Morose, a blonde, blue-eyed prostitute whose husband Martin was a cattle thief hiding out across the river in Juarez. Upon learning that Hardin and his wife had become lovers, the enraged, jealous husband tried to sneak back into El Paso but died in a wild barrage of gunfire on the Mexican Central Railway Bridge late at night on June 21, 1895. Martin Morose was probably lured to his death by a group including Deputy United States Marshal George Scarborough, Constable John Selman, former Chief of Police Jeff Milton, and Wes Hardin. When he was killed Morose was carrying $3700, money which Wes kept and refused to divide with the others; the bitter John Selman, an old gunfighter himself, was heard to complain, ". . . He has to come across or I'll kill him."

While Hardin was on a binge in Phenix, New Mexico, the wild and rowdy Beulah was staggering in a drunken stupor on the El Paso streets on the night of August 2. When she confronted policeman John Selman, Jr., on San Antonio Street, challenged him to a shooting match, and cursed him, the peace officer arrested her for carrying a gun. The next morning the contrite Beulah paid a fifty-dollar fine and apologized to the young officer. When Wes returned from Phenix, he seemed unconcerned about the arrest of his woman; in fact, he twice exchanged pleasant greetings with the younger Selman when the two met face-to-face. On the night of August 5, the tipsy Hardin beat Beulah during a quarrel and threatened to kill her before he passed out on the bed. After landlady Williams swore out a warrant for his arrest and Wes was put under a peace bond, Mrs. Morose finally left him and moved to Phoenix, Arizona.

On the evening of August 19, 1895, Hardin told friends that his story would be ended with one more day's work, then headed for the Acme Saloon. Among those he rolled dice with that fateful night was John Selman, Sr., who left the saloon about 9:00 PM after having several drinks. Shortly after eleven o'clock Wes was rolling dice at the bar with his back to the saloon front door. He had just remarked, "You have four sixes to beat," to grocer H. S. Brown when Constable Selman stepped through the saloon doors and fired four shots. The first bullet struck Wes in the head and killed him; after missing with his second shot, Selman stood over the prostrate Hardin and fired twice more, hitting him in the right arm and breast.

Both the motive for killing Hardin and the circumstances surrounding his death are disputed. There are two plausible reasons for Selman wanting to kill him. The accepted, historical version is the story told by Constable Selman at the inquest. He claimed that Hardin was so angered by the arrest of his woman that he threatened to kill John Selman, Jr. His dad stood up for the young officer and challenged Wes to a duel, an offer that was first declined before the two had their final confrontation in the Acme Saloon. However, the pleasantries exchanged between Hardin and the younger John Selman, Jr., and the two-week lapse of time between Beulah's arrest and the Acme saloon showdown would seem to indicate another, less honorable motive: Constable Selman was simply seeking revenge for not getting his cut of Martin Morose's money.

Then, there is the question as to Hardin's death. Selman steadfastly held to his story that Wes went for his gun first and that he was looking Hardin in the eye when he shot him. Taking into account both the conflicting testimony of witnesses and the clean bullet hole in Hardin's left eye, one must assume that he was *not* shot in the back of the head — the standard explanation for his death. To the contrary, the available evidence points to the following scenario: Wes Hardin probably saw some sort of warning sign in the bar mirror; he reached for his pistol with his right hand as he started to wheel around; the weapon stuck in the tight waistband of his pants and was only partially drawn by the time he was facing Selman; the two gunfighters *did* stand eye to eye for a split second before Selman fired his first fatal shot.*

The El Paso police phoned Fred Duderstadt, who gave the news to the Hardin children and convinced them that their father would not want his body returned to Gonzales. A funeral procession of only two carriages and two buggies followed Wes's body to the Concordia Cemetery at El Paso where he was buried in an unmarked grave one plot over from Martin Morose. The plate on Hardin's casket bore the words, "At Peace," a goal the forty-two-year-old gunman could achieve only in death. A manuscript was found in his personal papers; this autobiography which he wrote in the last year of his life was published by Smith and Moore of Seguin, Texas, in 1896.

Controversy continued to swirl around John Wesley Hardin even in death. As the years went by, the older graves in Concordia Cemetery were abandoned by caretakers; finally, in 1958, the city of El Paso built a wall around old Concordia to hide it from public view. Hardin's grave had no marker or mound and two successive caretakers seemed determined to keep the location a secret out of fear of vandals and souvenir hunters.

In July 1943 C.L. Sonnichsen, the noted "grassroots"

---

* John Selman, Sr., was charged with the murder of John Wesley Hardin but his trial resulted in a hung jury on February 12, 1896, with the jury favoring acquittal by a 10–2 margin. The case was rescheduled for the next term of the district court but Selman was dead by then. On April 5, 1896, he was shot four times by George Scarborough and died of his wounds the next day. Ironically, the motive for this killing was also the long-simmering argument over the splitting of Martin Morose's money.

Western historian, visited Smiley, Texas, while researching the old Sutton–Taylor Feud. There he met Elmer Spellman, whose wife was a granddaughter of Hardin, and learned of Wes's sister, "Aunt Mattie" Smith of Fort Worth. Spellman told Sonnichsen that the family wanted to put a marker on Hardin's grave and asked for his help in the project. However, Sonnichsen found Caretaker William R. Walker to be so hostile to the idea that nothing was accomplished for fifteen years. When Walker retired, Sonnichsen and Spellman met the new caretaker, Tom Dooley, in July 1959. A breakthrough came when Dooley pulled out some old, yellowed records and a map and took them to the location of the Hardin grave, hoping that the family would choose to move the body.

On November 19, 1962, the State National Bank of El Paso attached a bronze marker to the wall of the Lerner's ladies-wear store, the site of the old Acme Saloon where Hardin died. Then on September 29, 1965, twenty years of frustration ended for Sonnichsen and the Hardin family when a granite-and-bronze marker was placed over Wes Hardin's grave. In keeping with family wishes, it was a simple marker like that of Jane Hardin, containing only his name and dates. Even the laying of the marker was kept a secret for another four months. Today a steady stream of visitors come to the abandoned part of old Concordia Cemetery to pay homage at the grave of a legend.

VIII

Roy Bean:
Barroom Judge and Con Man

"By gobs, that's my rulin'!" These words brought twenty years of law and order to a huge frontier area west of the Pecos River after 1882. Justice of the Peace Roy Bean was *the* law in a wild and dangerous region two hundred miles from the nearest court of justice. He was part buffoon, clown wit and jester but there was no appeal from his decisions on murders, accidental deaths, suicides, assaults, cattle-rustling, horse thievery, drunkenness and inquests. At a time in Texas history when killings and shootouts were considered "affairs of honor," common sense governed many of his eccentric rulings. Judge Bean owned only one law book, could barely read and write, and made no pretense of knowing about rules of evidence or procedure, yet he was able to intimidate the toughest desperado in his combination courtroom–saloon. On the whole the influence of this dirty, profane, egotistical and overbearing "Law West of the Pecos" was beneficial. Even today his name is sure to surface when funny tales of the Texas bench are swapped. He cheated scores of its passengers but the Southern Pacific Railroad considered Roy a company asset. But how did Roy Bean become a living legend and nationally-known figure?

Judge Roy Bean and family at Langtry, Texas
Courtesy Western History Collections,
University of Oklahoma Library

Judge Roy Bean holding court
Courtesy Western History Collections,
University of Oklahoma Library

Judge Roy Bean on a horse
Courtesy Western History Collections,
University of Oklahoma Library

The youngest of three sons, he was born in Mason County, Kentucky, in 1825. His parents, Francis and Anna, were dirt poor and among the poor relations of a Bean family whose Maryland members had fought in the American Revolution and the War of 1812. Roy grew up determined to be "somebody important" like his older brothers; Joshua was to be the first mayor of San Diego and a major general in the California state militia while Sam became the first sheriff of Dona Ana County, New Mexico Territory. When he was sixteen the kid brother made a flatboat trip to New Orleans in the company of a gambler, got in trouble there and fled to San Antonio where brother Sam was a teamster hauling freight to Chihuahua City, Mexico. Roy later claimed that he drove an ammunition wagon for General Zachary Taylor during the Mexican War. In 1848 the two Bean brothers opened a trading post at Chihuahua. Shortly thereafter, Roy shot and killed his first man, a Mexican desperado who had waved a machete and shouted that he was going to kill a gringo. The local populace considered the killing an act of murder so the brothers fled to Jesus Maria in northern Sonora. In the spring of 1849, Roy moved on to San Diego, California, and a reunion with his oldest brother Joshua. Josh had first gone there in 1846, served as a captain in the regular army during the Mexican War, then was elected as first mayor of San Diego in 1850.

By then Roy stood five feet, ten inches tall and weighed 190 pounds. When the dark, handsome, strutting newcomer began to compete for the attention of the lovely San Diego senoritas, a tall blond Scotchman named Collins challenged him to a pistol shooting match on galloping horses; Roy accepted and chose the targets — each other! Sheriff Harathzy marked off a place on the main street and in the ensuing duel fought February 24, 1852, Collins was wounded in the right arm. Under pressure from an indignant citizenry, the sheriff arrested both men and they were charged with assault with intent to murder. For two months beautiful admirers sent flowers, food, wine and cigars to the jailed Roy, their last gift being a plate of knives encased by steaming hot tamales. He then dug his way through the cobblestone and concrete cell wall, mounted a waiting horse, and escaped on April 17, 1852.

Brother Josh was operating the Headquarters Saloon at San Gabriel, nine miles from Los Angeles, so Roy headed in that direction and became a bartender. After Josh became involved with a lady friend of the bandit Joaquin Murietta, he was murdered in November 1852 and Roy inherited the saloon. Now somebody important, he began to dress in a lavish Mexican costume with a pair of revolvers on his belt and a knife in one boot. However, his good fortune vanished in late 1854 when a pretty young senorita was kidnapped and forced to marry a Mexican officer. Roy was also a suitor of the young lady so challenged the officer to a duel and killed him. Six of the dead officer's friends then formed a hanging party with Roy the honoree and mounted him on his horse. The horse sensed the danger and moved away slowly, the rope stretched, and Bean was left dangling but barely touching the ground. When the avengers rode away, the senorita dashed out from behind a tree and cut the rope. Roy's senses returned a few minutes later but the injury left him with a rope burn red mark for life and a permanent stiff neck tilted to one side. This close call with death marred his appearance and caused him to leave California.

Sam Bean described Roy as "practically naked" when he showed up in 1858 at Mesilla, New Mexico, near Las Cruces where Sam was sheriff of Dona Ana County and ran a combination store, cafe, saloon and hotel. During the Civil War Roy claimed he served as a spy and scout under the command of Colonel John R. Baylor and organized a Confederate company called the Free Rovers

159

at Mesilla. After a Texas army invasion of New Mexico stalled after the Battle of Glorietta Pass in March 1862, Roy emptied Sam's safe, took his saddle horse, and joined the Texans as they retreated to San Antonio. For the duration of the war, he engaged in blockade running by hauling cotton from San Antonio to British ships off Matamoros, then returning with supplies.

Roy was to live in San Antonio for twenty years with the basic occupation of teamster. He felt at home in the Spanish atmosphere of the city and on October 28, 1866, married eighteen-year-old Virginia Chavez, a refined and cultured lady whose Spanish family traced their ancestry to the Canary Island founders of the city. They were to have two boys and two girls during a rocky, tempestuous married life; within a year her quick-tempered husband was hauled into court for aggravated assault and threatening the life of Virginia. The Bean family lived for sixteen years on South Flores Street in a poverty-stricken Mexican slum area called Beanville. Roy first tried the firewood business, using a stand of timber owned by a total stranger as his inventory. He then turned to the dairy business but could not resist the temptation to water his milk; when a local judge found a minnow in his milk, Roy explained that one of his cows must have swallowed it when drinking at the river. While he was a butcher, Roy's beef supply came from unbranded cattle belonging to area ranchers.

By the late 1870s he was operating a saloon on the south bank of the Medina River and freighting goods to Chihuahua by way of Presidio or El Paso. His teamster rig was so delapidated by 1880 that a Uvalde customer called Roy's equipment "a comical sight" and "the sorriest he ever beheld." His fortunes seemed to have struck rock bottom when N. W. Monroe, a friend and grading contractor for the Southern Pacific Railroad, suggested that Roy open a saloon at one of the construction camps then building west. Mrs. T. E. Connor, the wife of a prominent store owner in Beanville, was so anxious to have this unscrupulous character out of the neighborhood that she gave him nine hundred dollars for all his possessions on condition that he leave San Antonio. By then Roy and Virginia were separated; she later divorced him and remarried so he left his children with friends, Mr. and Mrs. Simon Fest, Jr., and embarked at age fifty-six on a promising new career.

At this time the Southern Pacific was building east from El Paso using Chinese laborers while the Gulf, Harrisburg and San Antonio Railway was building west from San Antonio with a crew of Canadian Irishmen. Roy used his cash grubstake to purchase a tent, ten fifty-five-gallon barrels of whiskey, canned goods, crackers, sardine and salmon cases, and some dry goods. Heading west toward the end of the tracks, he found himself just across the Pecos River by the spring of 1882. His first stop was a tent city which he named Vinegaroon after the vicious-looking creature with a stinger in its needle-like tail. That summer there were 8,000 workers within a twenty mile stretch of land at the juncture of the two railroads. Texas Ranger Captain Oglesby described the men building the line as "the worst lot of roughs, gamblers, robbers, and pickpockets collected here I ever saw." Since the nearest court of justice was two hundred miles away at Fort Stockton, the county seat, Captain Oglesby sent a letter to Adjutant General W.H. King at Austin on July 5, 1882, requesting a local law jurisdiction to clean up the construction camps. Roy Bean was in the right place at the right time; on August 2, 1882, the Commissioners Court of Pecos County appointed him as justice of the peace for Precinct Number Six with headquarters at Vinegaroon.

After first shooting up the saloon shack of a Jewish competitor, Roy opened his combination tent saloon and courtroom at Vinegaroon. It was there that he first called himself the "Law West of the Pecos" and backed up the claim with a few Rangers. His only guide was one law-book, the *Revised Statutes of Texas* [1879], preserved today at Langtry with its pages pencil-marked and dog-eared. From the beginning he made no attempt to keep up with new statutes and used newer books to "light fires with." At Vinegaroon Judge Bean started his practice of not allowing hung juries or appeals and of pocketing his fines to make his court self-sustaining. The earliest of his legendary rulings occurred there when Paddy O'Rourke, an Irish railroad foreman, accidentally killed a Chinese laborer. In a spirit of innocent fun, Paddy pulled his gun and told the Chinaman to duck; the hapless victim was shot when he failed to do so. The heavy-drinking Irish-men were good customers but Roy had little use for the thrifty Chinese, who preferred their own opium to his li-quor. In short, he knew where his business came from. Bean may also have been influenced by two hundred angry Irishmen who surrounded his saloon and threat-ened to lynch him if Paddy did not go free. When the ac-cused gunman was brought before him, the judge thumbed through his law book and judiciously an-nounced that homicide was the killing of a human being; however, he could find no law against killing a China-man so he dismissed the case and ordered a round of drinks courtesy of the grateful Paddy.

By December 1882, the tracks had passed Vinega-roon and the tent city began to disappear so Roy decided to take his law and saloon seventy miles west to Straw-bridge (now Sanderson), a division point on the railroad line. When he arrived he found a thriving saloon already there owned by a big Irishman named Charlie Wilson. After Roy opened his business, Charlie sent a Mexican to the Bean saloon in the dead of night with orders to pour kerosene into the whiskey barrel. With his liquor supply tainted and his customers driven off, the judge admitted defeat and retreated to a place called Eagle's Nest twenty miles west of the Pecos River. A water tank was being built there and a town site being laid out by Jesus Torres, whose father owned the land. This town site was soon to be renamed Langtry by the Southern Pacific in honor of George Langtry, the civil engineer in charge of surveying the El Paso division of the line. Torres already operated the Eagle's Nest Saloon on the south side of the tracks; when he gave 640 acres to the railroad contingent on a station being built, a clause in the contract stated that no lot, plot or tract of land within Langtry could be sold, leased or granted to his competitor, Roy Bean. Paddy O'Rourke solved this problem for Roy by telling him to pitch his saloon tent on the railroad right-of-way, which was not a part of the town plot. The Southern Pacific was agreeable to this scheme and the judge squatted on land he had no legal right to claim for the next twenty years.

Langtry was the perfect location for Bean. After the tracks joined at Dead Man's Canyon on January 12, 1883, train service connected New Orleans and San Francisco. The engines stopped for water at Langtry, giving thirsty passengers twenty minutes to stretch their legs and buy a drink. Roy first built a small frame shack with a covered porch on the north side of the tracks, then Bean sentenced a sign-painter he had arrested for disturbing the peace to work off the fine by painting the following signs over the establishment:

THE JERSEY LILLY
SALOON
COURT HOUSE
JUDGE ROY BEAN
THE LAW WEST OF THE PECOS
JUSTICE OF THE PEACE
WHISKEY, WINE AND BEER

Bean named his saloon—courtroom "The Jersey Lilly" in honor of Lillie Langtry, England's most beauti-

163

ful and notorious actress. When Roy first saw a full-page picture of her in the *London Illustrated News,* he is reported to have exclaimed, "By gobs! Ziggity! What a purty critter!" He put the picture on his saloon wall behind the judge's bench and developed a long-distance, almost worshipful admiration for Lillie. In a spirit of fun, he wrote her telling that he had named *his* town and a saloon in her honor. She received the letter in the winter of 1883–1884 while on a United States tour. Deeply touched, she replied that she could not visit the town but wished to present an ornamental drinking fountain for the town square to show her appreciation. Roy was quick to reply that "it would be quite useless, as the only thing the citizens of Langtry did not drink was water." The two never met but the judge, dressed in his best plug hat and Prince Albert jacket, was in the audience during two of Lillie's performances at San Antonio on April 20 and 21,

---

Emily Charlotte LeBreton, the daughter of a clergyman, was born on the Isle of Jersey and married Edward Langtry at age twenty-two. She was first called "The Jersey Lily" by John S. Sargent when he painted a portrait of her; the title stayed with Lillie until her death in February 1929. When he first saw this auburn-haired, blue-eyed lady, the poet Oscar Wilde called her "the most beautiful woman in the world." For a time Lillie was the mistress of the Prince of Wales, the future King Edward VII. During the liaison he gave her a house and showered Lillie with clothes and jewels; the baby she had in France, Jeanne-Marie, was rumored to be the Prince's but was really the offspring of his favorite nephew, Louis Battenberg.

After separating from her alcoholic husband, Lillie became an actress simply because she needed money. Her first American tour started at New York in October 1882 and the play broke box office records. Her notoriety increased after she started a torrid romance with young Freddie Gebhard, a rich American playboy. Freddie paid $250,000 for a specially-built private railway car for Lillie's transcontinental tour in the spring of 1887. The car was seventy-five feet long and had a white roof, blue exterior, and wreaths of golden lillies painted on the sides; the interior contained Lillie's own bedroom and two others for guests, a bath with silver fixtures, a parlor with a piano, and a kitchen. After she and Freddie purchased a California ranch in 1887, Lillie became a United States citizen as a ploy to obtain an American divorce. She further scandalized Victorian America in 1903 when she starred in the play, "Mrs. Deering's Divorce," and took off her dress to reveal a full-length slip.

164

1888. When she departed, a Texas reporter was inspired to say, "Farewell, oh langorous Lily. San Antonio has seen, admired, devoured with its eyes. San Antonio has paid . . . Rest assured that we have had our money's worth." When he returned to Langtry, Bean began to trim his mustache like that of the Prince of Wales, Lillie's former lover, and continued to be enamored of her; in December 1902, only months before his death, he sent her a wild turkey for Christmas.

Roy soon brought his four children — Roy Jr., Laura, Zulema and Sam — from San Antonio to live with him in the Jersey Lilly. To the left of the entrance was his store; to the right was the bar and courtroom. Daughters Laura and Zulema roomed directly behind the bar, Sam slept on a pool table in the center, and the judge bunked in a rear corner. The place was usually filthy and cluttered with papers and magazines; Roy wanted his customers to think that he liked to read. Both girls were quite attractive, fine horsewomen, and were treated as ladies by area cowhands. They eventually married Southern Pacific bridge foremen and, as widows, lived next to each other in New Orleans. Only Sam, the youngest of the Bean children, would remain at home with his father.

Judge Bean derived his power solely as a justice of the peace. First appointed for a two year term in 1882, he was elected to that office in 1884, then saw his domain reduced in 1885 when Val Verde County was created with Del Rio as county seat. After he was defeated for office in 1886, the Commissioners Court in February 1887 created a new justice precinct which included all of the county west of the Pecos River and appointed Roy as justice of the peace. Even after Jesus Torres defeated him in 1896, Bean refused to surrender his seal and law book and continued to try all cases north of the tracks.

"Hear ye! Hear ye! This honorable court is now in session, and if anybody wants a snort before we start, step up to the bar and name your poison." These words and the Judge's booming voice and overbearing manner struck fear in the hearts of horse thieves, cattle rustlers, and crooked gamblers in Roy's jurisdiction. Since there was no jail in Langtry, all cases were considered fineable offenses and the Rangers chained defendants by their ankles to an old mesquite as an overnight lockup. When asked by the state attorney why he did not remit the state's part of fees collected, Roy replied that his court had to be self-sustaining and suggested that each should tend to his own judicial business. The judge used each Monday to clear his docket and pocket the fees. Prisoners were forced to stand erect at attention during trials and knew that there was no appeal from his decisions. Any juror appointed by the judge had to be a good bar customer and was expected to have a drink (or two) during every court recess. Roy fined drunks the exact amount in their pockets and was likely to let a horse thief go free if the horses were recovered. After 1890 Bean used his judicial powers to boost his saloon business with many trials becoming little more than a good excuse for a collective drinking binge. However, he did sentence at least two men to be hanged and the execution of Carlos Robles, a Mexican cattle rustler, was actually carried out. The other case involved a young thief who had taken a roadmaster's wallet and six-shooter. When brought before the "bar of justice," he unleased a string of profanities and tried to cut Sam Bean with a knife. Roy shouted that he would shut up the young man with a rope, the jury found him guilty, and the judge delivered the death sentence. After the noose was placed around his neck and the rope thrown across a box car, storekeeper Billy Dodd slipped it off and told the thoroughly chastised young man to "run like hell." After the ruckus was over, Judge Bean remarked that the scare had been a good lesson for the thief.

A Bean wedding was a five-dollar affair; if the husband did not have the money, he could work out the fee.

The climax to the ceremony came when the judge told the couple to hold up their right hands, then pronounced them man and wife with the concluding words," . . . and may God have mercy on your souls." Once when two married Mexicans became involved with each other's wives and family honor became an issue, Roy's solution was to grant two divorces, switch couples, remarry them, then send the newlyweds in opposite directions on the next trains. He summed up his actions by stating that he had done a good day's deed for suffering humanity. When the rumor reached El Paso that Roy was granting divorces, a function of district courts only, he defended the practice by telling District Judge T. A. Falvey that since he married couples, he had the right to unmarry them if it didn't take; he was "just rectifying an error" and would continue to do so. Once when he was asked about his divorces, Roy slapped his pocket, winked and said, "If they won't team up, let 'em carry single." His "divorce mill" carried a ten-dollar fee.

Another favorite chore of the judge was to officiate as coroner and conduct inquests for the five-dollar fee. He had a field day in 1892 while the Pecos River high bridge was under construction. Ten carpenters fell three hundred feet to their death on the canyon floor when some bridge timbers gave way. After looking first at the corpses and then at the wreckage of heavy beams, Bean's inquest ruling was that each of the workers had been killed by the falling timbers. Another legendary ruling of Judge Bean occurred in February 1892 when a bridge carpenter named Pat O'Brien died when blown off the Myers Canyon bridge by a gust of wind. When the body was brought to the Jersey Lilly, Roy found a six-shooter and forty dollars on the corpse, then proceeded to fine the defendant that amount for carrying a concealed weapon; to the judge's way of thinking, forty dollars would provide for a proper Christian burial. Another time when Bean saw a bullet hole in the forehead of a mouldering

Mexican skull, he ruled that the victim "met his death by being shot by a person unknown who was a damn good shot."

Roy Bean made a small fortune from the Southern Pacific Railroad. Once a boxcar loaded with sugar turned over on a bridge west of Langtry. As news of the derailment spread, many locals rushed to the site to fill sacks and buckets with the scarce delicacy. Bean, on the other hand, arrived at the scene of the looting with a helper, shovels, and a wagon, then proceeded to cart off a year's supply of sugar to be sold in his store. When a train killed one of his donkeys, the judge wrote a letter requesting fifteen hundred dollars to compensate for the loss of his "prize Kentucky jack." Even after a local railroad employee pointed out that the old, blind burro might be worth fifty cents, the Southern Pacific awarded Roy five hundred dollars. Trains stopped at Langtry for ten to twenty minutes, enough time for a quick visit to the Jersey Lilly, and the judge never gave back change for his thirty-five cent warm bottled beer. If a customer protested too vigorously or too long, he might be fined for disturbing the peace and miss the departing train. One New Yorker lost a twenty-dollar gold piece in this manner while another from the same state asked for iced beer and was told by Roy, "Well who in the hell ever heard of ice in Texas in July." A favorite trick played on passengers with more refined tastes was to keep a lump of glass on hand, then drop it into a cocktail to produce a tinkling ice-like sound when the drink was stirred. Another ploy involved not taking the passenger's money until the train whistle blew, then dropping and "losing" the change. As word of his antics spread, Roy became a great tourist attraction and always sat on the front porch of the Jersey Lilly at train time to be seen by the curious. It must have been an unforgettable sight, this old man wearing a Mexican sombrero with the tobacco-stained gray beard and the potbelly hanging over his belt. Thousands of tourists visited the Jersey Lilly in the 1890s while Roy would periodically clean up, put on his Prince Albert coat and plug hat, and use his yearly pass to meet with railroad officials at San Antonio or El Paso.

When Judge Bean learned that Jay Gould and his party would pass through Langtry on a special train in 1890, he ordered a case of champagne from San Antonio and used his red handkerchief to flag down the train engineer; seeing the danger signal and assuming that a bridge was out, the engineer came to an unscheduled halt. Roy sauntered to the car window and invited Gould, his daughter Helen, and their party to visit the Jersey Lilly as his guests. The famed financier accepted and provided ladyfingers to eat while the ladies asked so many questions about the judge's pets and duties that the train was delayed for two hours. This delay resulted in a report going out to the effect that Gould had been killed in a train wreck and caused a brief panic on the New York Stock Exchange. From that time on, Roy Bean liked to speak of "my friend Jay Gould."

Any beer or whiskey drummer who made a business call at the Jersey Lilly was expected to set up drinks for the house, then count the empty bottles to settle his bill. Roy even made a racket out of this by keeping a supply of old empties under the bar to count in with the rest. Complaining about his liquor could be dangerous. After a rowdy cowboy rode his pony into the Jersey Lilly, demanded a "drink of pure pizen," and turned down Roy's best whiskey as being "rainwater," the judge reached for a jar of embalmed tarantulas and poured that alcohol into a glass. He ordered the cowboy to drink it at gunpoint, then let the ashen-faced customer off the hook by demanding that he buy drinks for the house. The judge even used a pet brown bear named Bruno to help sell liquor. By day the bear was chained to Bean's front porch corner post; by night he was chained to Roy's bedpost. A quick way to get a drunk sober enough to appear in court was to chain him and Bruno to the same post! The pet soon developed a taste for beer and could hold it better than any human; many a customer at the Jersey Lilly bought a beer, then threw the bottle to Bruno and watched as he pulled the loosened cork out with his teeth. However, his master's no-change racket brought an end to the bear. During a train stop a lawyer named Will James gave Roy a twenty-dollar gold piece for two bottles of beer and was given eighty-five cents change. His strong complaints caused the judge to fine James $6.66 on each of three counts: disturbing the peace, abusive language and contempt of court. The lawyer had his revenge a few weeks later when he returned from El Paso and saw Roy in the bar of the Menger Hotel at San Antonio. After telling the judge that Bruno was dead, he asked for the bear's hide to mount in his den. The gullible Bean wrote out a telegram on the spot telling his son Sam to skin Bruno and ship the hide to the lawyer. When he returned to Langtry, the judge was outraged to find that his beloved bear had died from a dose of Sam's buckshot. The younger Bean defended his actions by exclaiming, "I couldn't skin him alive, could I?"

The most profitable day of Roy Bean's business career occurred on February 21, 1896, when he staged the Fitzsimmons–Maher heavyweight championship fight. Dallas was to have been the site of the bout until the Texas legislature was called into special session by Governor Charles Culberson and passed a law making it a felony to hold a prize fight in the state. Promoter Dan Stuart then announced that the fight would be held "in or near El Paso" after some businessmen offered him a $6,000 bonus to choose their wide-open city. The fight date was to be Valentine's Day and with Mexico, Arizona and New Mexico nearby, Stuart could keep the exact location of the contest a secret until the last minute. However, the match seemed doomed after the United States Congress eliminated Arizona and New Mexico as sites by outlawing "pugilistic encounters" in the territories. To make matters worse, three companies of Texas Rangers rode into El Paso thirty-six hours before the contest with orders to stop it. Roy Bean saw his chance and on February 15, 1896, sent a telegram from Langtry inviting Stuart to bring the fight there with a guarantee of no interference; at the same time the judge ordered a carload of beer from San Antonio. Stuart jumped at the offer and sold three hundred round trip tickets on two special trains which pulled into Langtry at 3:00 P.M. on February 21. Eighteen Rangers were sent to stop the prize fight but when they confronted Roy, he informed them that the contest would be held on the Mexican side of the river where the Texas Rangers had no jurisdiction. The bamboozled lawmen were then invited to cool off, relax and enjoy the fight. After downing one-dollar-a-bottle beer at the Jersey Lilly, the passengers crossed a pontoon bridge over the Rio Grande to a ring built on a sandy flat in the bottom of a canyon in the state of Coahuila, Mexico. There was a canvas wall around the ring and two hundred fight fans paid twenty dollars each to stand and view the spectacle. The fight started at 4:15 P.M. and ended in a knockout one minute and thirty-five seconds later with a Fitzsimmons short right hook to Maher's jaw. After another round of Bean beer, the passengers boarded their trains and were off, leaving Roy behind to count his considerable change.

In January 1898 Sam Bean was involved in a shooting which took much of the spark out of his father. After a Mr. Upshaw made fun of Sam's Mexican blanket, the two went at it with their fists with Sam coming out the loser. He then rushed into the saloon, grabbed his rifle, and shot Upshaw in the back. Sam was indicted for murder by a grand jury in Del Rio and stood trial from September until March 1899. Mrs. Trent, the wife of the station agent, had observed the killing but her testimony was disallowed because she saw the incident through a glass window. During the long trial Roy's beard turned white from anxiety and he paid a heavy price in lawyers' fees and lost business even though Sam was ultimately acquitted. The final blow came when the judge went home after the trial to find the Jersey Lilly burned to the ground. It was to be replaced by the one-room structure that stands today.

A Langtry native, Mrs. Beulah Birdwell Farley, said that "Roy Bean might have been a murderer and a robber and a thief, but he was a good man in his way." Most of Roy's profits in his last years went to care for hungry tramps or to buy medicine and food for the destitute Mexicans of the area. Widows of the community who could not fend for themselves had their firewood supplied by the judge. He did his part to promote the education of the children of Langtry by keeping a large stack of heating wood behind the schoolhouse each winter. However, it would seem that the local schoolmarms did not return his interest; one teacher was so repulsed by the food particles and tobacco juice on Roy's beard that she refused to eat at the same rooming house table with him.

Judge Falvey, who presided over the district from Del Rio to El Paso, said of Roy Bean:

> That man did a world of good. He was the man for the place. The rough community where he had settled would have tolerated no enforcement of the law as it was printed on the statute books. But they tolerated Bean because he was both law and equity, right and justice. He filled a place that could not have been filled by any other man. He was distinctly a creation of circumstances.
>
> He was in control of the situation and his control was the only one possible. His decisions were not only always according to the law and the fact, but they were accepted, and that was the big point. He was what he claimed to be, the Law West of the Pecos.

Early in 1903 Roy learned that Lillie Langtry was again on tour in the United States and would be perform-

172

ing in both San Antonio and El Paso; she would be passing through his town at last! For a time his spirits revived as he rushed plans for her grand reception but then his health began to fail. After hearing of a power company's plan to build a dam on the Pecos, he began to drink more, lost interest in his saloon, and told his friend Billy Dodd that the country had moved along and left him, and they were "crushin' the spirit of the Pecos." A prolonged drinking binge at Del Rio led to heart and lung complications and the seventy-eight-year-old Bean died in his saloon on March 16, 1903, with Sam at his side. Two days later he was buried in the Del Rio cemetery. Sam started but never finished a book about the judge, was stabbed to death in a barroom brawl at Del Rio in 1907, and was buried beside his dad.

The spirit of Judge Roy Bean in his prime was best summed up when the governor of Texas reprimanded him for taking over the functions of a district judge and exceeding his authority. Roy replied by telling the governor to run things at Austin any way he liked but that *he* was the "Law West of the Pecos, by gobs, and that's my rulin'!" In 1939 the Texas Legislature acquired his old saloon and directed the Texas Highway Department to restore and perpetually preserve the "Jersey Lilly." Bean's spirit is kept alive today through the Judge Roy Bean Visitor Center at Langtry. In 1981 more than 80,000 people viewed dioramas with sound and tools of the famed judge's trade on display at the center.

There is a postscript to this story. At 6:00 P.M. on January 4, 1904, the Southern Pacific's *Sunset Express* train stopped at Langtry; at the far end of the train was Lillie Langtry's ornate private railway car. A large crowd surged forward to see the plump but still curvaceous Lillie step outside. Justice Billy Dodd, Roy's successor, served as master of ceremonies to welcome her, saying that "it would have been the proudest day in the late King's life if he had lived to meet her." After a round of speeches, everyone adjourned to the Jersey Lilly saloon where Lillie heard some Bean anecdotes and cut a deck of cards "for luck." In her book, *The Days I Knew*, she later described the saloon thusly:

> I found it a roughly built wooden two-story house, its entire front being shaded by a piazza, on which a chained monkey gambolled, . . . The interior of the 'Ritz' of Langtry consisted of a long, narrow room, which comprised the entire ground floor, whence a ladder stair-case led to a sleeping-loft. One side of the room was given up to a bar, . . . while stoutly made tables and a few benches occupied the vacant space. The tables showed plainly that they had been severely used, for they were slashed as if with bowie knives, . . .

The Bean tales Lillie heard on this "short but unforgettable visit" led her to note that "the stories of his ready wit and audacity made me indeed sorry that he had not lived over my visit." After seeing several cages on her special car, some cowboys tried to gift Lillie with one of Roy's pets, a huge cinnamon bear, but the creature escaped after being tied to the train platform. As a substitute, she was later given Roy's old six-shooter, which was to hang in a place of honor in her England home. The famed fifty-one-year-old actress was in Bean's town for thirty minutes before the train departed for El Paso.

The next day the caretaker at the Del Rio cemetery discovered that the ground above Roy's grave had shifted. Langtry residents had a ready explanation for this eerie phenomenon: Bean was so frustrated at missing Lillie's visit that he turned over in his grave!

I

Brit Bailey and Strap Buckner:
Legendary Characters of Early Texas

Suggested Sources for Further Reading:

Brown, John Henry. *History of Texas from 1685 to 1892*. 2 vols. fac. Austin: Pemberton Press, 1970.

Creighton, James. *A Narrative History of Brazoria County*. Angleton: Brazoria County Historical Commission, 1975.

Dobie, J. Frank. *The Flavor of Texas*. Austin: Jenkins, 1975.

Foster, Catherine Munson. *Ghosts Along The Brazos*. Waco: Texian Press, 1977.

Rust, Jr., Mrs. George. "Genealogical Record." Unpublished Manuscript. Wharton, Texas, n.d.

Stroebel, Abner. *The Old Plantations and Their Owners of Brazoria County*. Houston: Union National Bank, 1926.

Syers, William. *Off the Beaten Trail*. Waco: Texian Press, 1972.

Weyand, Leonie Rummel and Houston Wade. *An Early History of Fayette County*. LaGrange: *LaGrange Journal*, 1936.

II

Josiah Wilbarger: The Man Who Survived His Scalping

Suggested Sources for Further Reading:

Dobie, J. Frank, ed. *Tales of Old-Time Texas*. Boston: Little Brown, 1955.

Jenkins, John Holmes, III, ed. *Recollections of Early Texas: The Memoirs of John Holland Jenkins*. Austin: The University of Texas Press, 1958.

Pickrell, Annie Doom. *Pioneer Women in Texas*. Austin: Jenkins, 1970.

Syers, William. *Off the Beaten Trail*. Waco: Texian Press, 1972.

Welch, June Rayfield. *People and Places in the Texas Past*. Dallas: G.L.A. Press, 1974.

Wilbarger, J.W. *Indian Depredations in Texas*. fac. Austin: Pemberton Press, 1967.

"Josiah Pugh Wilbarger, Pioneer." Unpublished Manuscript. Bastrop Public Library, n.d.

III
Pamelia Man: She Did It Her Way

Suggested Sources for Further Reading:

Bartholomew, Ed. *The Houston Story, 1836–1865*. Houston: Frontier Press of Texas, 1951.

Braider, Donald. *Solitary Star; a Biography of Sam Houston*. New York: G. P. Putnam's Sons, 1974.

Dobie, J. Frank. *The Flavor of Texas*. Austin: Jenkins, 1975.

Hogan, William Ransom. "Pamelia Mann, Texas Frontierswoman." *Southwest Review*, XX (Summer 1935), 360–370.

King, C. Richard. *Susanna Dickinson: Messenger of the Alamo*. Austin: Shoal Creek, 1976.

McComb, David. *Houston, The Bayou City*. Austin: The University of Texas Press, 1969.

Miller, Ray, *Ray Miller's Houston*. Austin: Capital Printing, 1982.

Stiff, Edward. *The Texan Emigrant*. fac. Waco: Texian Press, 1968.

Turner, Martha Anne. *Sam Houston and His Twelve Women; the Ladies Who Influenced the Life of Texas's Greatest Statesman*. Austin: Pemberton Press, 1966.

IV
Gail Borden: A Texas Success Story

Suggested Sources for Further Reading:

Barrington, Carol. "Go Down To Egypt Land." *Texas Highways*, June 1981, pp. 2–6.

Beals, Carleton. *Stephen F. Austin, Father of Texas*. New York: McGraw-Hill, 1953.

Frantz, Joe B. *Gail Borden, Dairyman to a Nation*. Norman: University of Oklahoma Press, 1951.

Hayes, Charles. *Galveston: History of the Island and the City*. 2 vols. Austin: Jenkins Garrett Press, 1974.

Silverthorne, Elizabeth. *Ashbel Smith of Texas: Pioneer, Patriot, Statesman, 1805–1886*. College Station: Texas A&M University Press, 1982.

Wharton, Clarence R. *Gail Borden, Pioneer*. San Antonio: Naylor, 1941.

Wisehart, Marion. *Sam Houston, American Giant*. Washington: R. B. Luce, 1962.

V

The Saga of Cynthia Ann and Quanah Parker

Suggested Sources for Further Reading:

Capps, Benjamin. *The Great Chiefs*. New York: Time–Life Books, 1975.

DeShields, James T. *Cynthia Ann Parker*. San Antonio: Naylor, 1934.

Fehrenbach, T. R. *Lone Star: A History of Texas and the Texans*. New York: MacMillan, 1968.

———. *Comanches: The Destruction of a People*. New York: Alfred Knopf, 1974.

Hagan, William. *United States-Comanche Relations: The Reservation Years*. New Haven and London: Yale Univ. Press, 1976.

Haley, James F. *The Buffalo War: The History of the Red River Indian Uprising of 1874*. New York: Doubleday, 1976.

Holt, Roy. *Heap Many Texas Chiefs*. San Antonio: Naylor, 1966.

Jackson, Grace. *Cynthia Ann Parker*. San Antonio: Naylor, 1959.

McCarty, John. *Adobe Walls Bride: The Story of Billy and Olive Dixon*. San Antonio: Naylor, 1955.

Mayhall, Mildred. *Indian Wars of Texas*. Waco: Texian Press, 1965.

Pinkard, Tommie. "They Come In Peace." (Parker Family Reunion) *Texas Highways*. October 1983, pp. 42–47.

Wallace, Ernest. *The Comanches: Lords of the South Plains*. Norman: Univ. of Oklahoma Press, 1952.

Welch, June Rayfield. *People and Places in the Texas Past*. Dallas: G.L.A. Press, 1974.

Wilbarger, J. W. *Indian Depredations in Texas*. fac. Austin: Pemberton Press, 1967.

Wood, Norman Barton. *Lives of Famous Indian Chiefs*. Chicago: L. W. Walter, 1906.

Battles of Texas. Waco: Texian Press, 1967.

VI

L. H. McNelly: The Ranger Who Kept on Coming

Suggested Sources for Further Reading:

Conger, Roger, ed. *Rangers of Texas*. Waco: Texian Press, 1969.

Durham, George. *Taming the Nueces Strip: the Story of McNelly's Rangers*. Austin: The Univ. of Texas Press, 1962.

Jennings, N. A. *A Texas Ranger*. fac. New York: Charles Scribner, 1899.

Keating, Bern. *An Illustrated History of the Texas Rangers*. Chicago: Rand McNally, 1975.

Lea, Tom. *The King Ranch*. 2 vols. Boston: Little, Brown & Co., 1957.

Mason, Herbert Molloy. *The Texas Rangers*. New York: Meredith Press, 1967.

Sterling, William. *Trails and Trials of a Texas Ranger*. Norman: University of Oklahoma Press, 1968.

Webb, Walter Prescott. *The Texas Rangers: a Century of Frontier Defense*. Austin: The Univ. of Texas Press, 1965.

Woodman, Lyman. *Cortina: Rogue of the Rio Grande*. San Antonio: Naylor, 1950.

VII
John Wesley Hardin: A Gunfighter and His Times

Suggested Sources for Further Reading:

Hardin, John Wesley. *The Life of John Wesley Hardin as Written by Himself*. fac. Norman: University of Oklahoma Press, 1961.

Metz, Leon. *John Selman, Gunfighter*. 2nd ed. Norman: University of Oklahoma Press, 1980.

Nordyke, Lewis. *John Wesley Hardin, Texas Gunman*. New York: Morrow, 1957.

Parsons, Chuck. *The Capture of John Wesley Hardin*. College Station: Creative Publishing Co., 1978

Ripley, Thomas. *They Died With Their Boots On*. Garden City, N.Y.: Doubleday, Doran and Co., 1935.

Sonnichsen, C. L. *I'll Die Before I Run: the Story of the Great Feuds of Texas*. New York: Devin–Adair Co., 1962.

———. *The Grave of John Wesley Hardin*. College Station: Texas A&M University Press, 1979.

Sutton, Robert C. *The Sutton–Taylor Feud*. Quanah: Nortex Press, 1974.

Trachtman, Paul. *The Gunfighters*. New York: Time–Life Books, 1974.

VIII
Roy Bean: Barroom Judge and Con Man

Suggested Sources for Further Reading:

Herr, Pamela. "Lillie on the Frontier." *The American West*, March/April 1981, pp. 40–45.

Lake, Stuart N. "Vinegarroon and the Jersey Lily." *Saturday Evening Post*, 7 February 1931.

Lloyd, Everett. *Law West of the Pecos: The Story of Roy Bean.* San Antonio: Naylor, 1936.

McDaniel, Ruel. *Vinegarroon: The Saga of Judge Roy Bean, "Law West of the Pecos."* Kingsport, Tenn.: Southern, 1936.

Sichel, Pierre. *The Jersey Lily; The Story of the Fabulous Mrs. Langtry.* Englewood Cliffs, N.J.: Prentice–Hall, 1958.

Sonnichsen, C. L. *Roy Bean: Law West of the Pecos.* New York: Devin–Adair Company, 1958.

INDEX

A

Abernathy, Jack, 92
Addison, Reverend O. M., 28, 39
Alexander, A. J., 115, 117
Allen, Sam, 27
Anderson, Dr., 24
Arapaho Indians, 81
Archer, Branch T., 7
Armstrong, John B., 108, 141, 142, 143, 144
Austin's Colony at Mina [Bastrop], 20
Austin,s Colony, 1, 5
Austin's Second Colony, 45
Austin, John, 7
    Stephen F., 1, 2, 11, 12, 13, 41, 43, 44, 47, 48, 51, 52

B

Bailey Children, 1
Bailey, Edith Smith, 1
    Elizabeth [see Milburn]
    Gaines, 8
    James Briton (Brit), 1–10, 15
    Margaret, 5
    Mary, [see Polley]
    Nancy, 5, 9
    Sarah, 5
    Smith, 8
Bailey's Ghost, 9–10
Bailey's Servant Jim, 10
Baker, Joseph, 48, 50
    Mosely, 49
    Parson, 61
Baladon [sic, Muldoon], 14
Barrickman, Alex, 139
Battenberg, Louis, 164
Battle of Jones Creek, 4
Battle of San Jacinto, 31
Battle of Velasco, 6, 8, 15
Baylor, John R., 159
Beall, Dr., 90
Bean, Anna, 158
    Francis, 158

Joshua, 158, 159
Judge Roy, 155–174
    Laura, 165
    Roy Jr., 165
    Sam, 158, 159, 160, 165, 166, 170, 171, 173
    Virginia (Chavez), 160, 161
    Zulema, 165
Beaumont, Eugene, 85
Belknap, Secretary of War, 117
Bell, Peter H., 60
Bent, William, 80
Bideno, Juan, 135
Billings, [Mr.], 146
Birdsong, A. C., 94
    Neda [Parker], 95
Borden, Gail, Jr., 41–67
    Gail, Sr., 41, 43, 44, 57, 66
    Augusta, 57, 63
    Demis (Woodward), 44
    Henry Lee, 66, 67
    John Gail, 57, 63, 66
    John P., 47, 49, 50, 51, 52, 66, 67
    Mary, 45, 47
    Paschal, 49
    Philadelphia (Wheeler), 41
    Penelope (Mercer), 44, 55, 57
    Thomas H., 43, 44, 47, 48, 50, 51, 53, 66, 67
    [Mrs. Thomas], 51
Bowen, Brown, 142, 144, 145, 146
    Jane [see Hardin], 133, 136, 137
    Neal, 142, 146
Boyd, (a trooper), 114
Bradburn, John Davis (Juan), 6, 7, 8, 53
Bradley, Jim, 131
Brazell, George, 122, 123
    Philip, 122, 123
Brazoria, 7, 8
Brown, H. S., 152

181

Henry S., 7
Mrs. John Henry, 77
Browne, Sheriff, 113
Bryce, Lord, 89, 90
"Bubba, Uncle," 9
Buckner, Aylett C. (Strap), 1, 7,
    10–15
    Elizabeth Lewis, 10
    Judge Aylett, 10
Burleson, Rufus C., 56
Burnet, David G., 49, 50
Burnett, Burk, 77, 89, 93
    Samuel Burk, 89
Bustamente, President, 8

C

Caddo Indians, 71, 72
Callicott, Bill, 118, 119
Campbell, Neal, 143
Capitol Hotel, 39
Carlisle Indian School, 93
Carol, Columbus, 134
Carrington, Dr., 137
Carter, Amon G., 77
Cavanaugh Family, 13
Chamberlain, Caroline, 111,
    119, 125
Chambers, Fenora, 17
    Margaret, [see Wilbarger],
    25
    Talbert C., 25
Chapman, Amos, 81
Charlton, John, 85
Chavez, Virginia, (see Bean),
    160
Cheyenne Indians, 81, 82, 83,
    85
Childress, George, 49
Chipley, William Dudley, 142,
    143, 144
Christian, Mr., 20, 21, 23
Church, Emeline Eunice, (Bor-
    den), 65
Clark, John, 45
    John C., 44
Clements Cousins, 133, 134
Clements Family, 138
    Jim, 133, 139
    Mannen, 133, 136, 137, 139,

146, 150
Clendenin, Major, 115
Clifton, Mrs. Margaret, 22, 23,
    24
Clinton, The [Steamer], 107,
    140
Coe, Phil, 132
Coke, Richard, 107, 108, 122,
    139
Cole, John P., 12
Coleman, Bob, 149, 150
    Robert, 28, 30
Collins, [Mr.], 158
Comanche food staple "Pinole,"
    58
Comanche Indians, 21, 26, 69,
    71, 72, 73, 74, 78, 79, 81,
    84, 85, 87, 88, 94
Comanche White House, The,
    89
Comanche–Kiowa Reserva-
    tion, 80, 89, 92
Comanchero, 84
Connor, Mrs. T. E., 160
Conrad, Charles, 59
Coran, Bill, 135
Corning, A. F., 77
Cortina, Juan, 109, 110, 112,
    119
Cox, James, 96
Cruger, Jacob W., 53
Culberson, Charles, 170
Cummins, James, 12
Cureton, Jack, 75
Currie, John, 62

D

Davidson, [the DA], 148
Davis, E. J., 105, 106, 132, 136,
    139
    Gaily Faith Parker, 96
Delaware Indians, 72
Dewees, W. B., 11
Diaz, Porfirio, 119
Dickinson, Susanna, 34
Dixon, Bill, 140
    Billy, 80, 82, 83, 84
    Bud, 141
    Mary Elizabeth [Hardin],

125
Simp, 131
Tom, 141
William, 128
Dixon Family Murders, 130
Dodd, Billy, 166, 173
Dona Juanita, 73
Donahue, William, 73
Dooley, Tom, 154
Duderstadt, Fred, 148, 149, 150, 153
Duncan, Jack, 108, 142, 143, 146
Durham, Caroline (see Chamberlain), 125
George (Josh), 108, 111, 112, 113, 118, 119, 121, 122, 124, 125

E

Edward VII, King, 164
Edwards, Benjamin, 13
Monroe, 7
Eighth Cavalry, 17
Evans, Mrs., 77

F

Falvey, T. A., 167, 172
Farley, Beulah Birdwell, 172
Fest, Mr. and Mrs. Simon, Jr., 161
Fisher, King (John), 120, 121, 122
Sarah Vivian, 121
Fitzsimmons, 171
Fitzsimmons–Maher fight, 170
Flores, Juan, 115, 116, 117, 120
Flowers Family, 13
Ford, John S. (Rip), 25, 75
Fort Marion, Florida, 86
Fort Velasco, 6, 7, 8, 15
Fourth Cavalry, 84
Franklin. B. C., 37
Frazer, G. A. (Bud), 150
Frost, Robert, 71
Samuel, 71

G

Garcia, Luciano, 3
Gates, John, 137

Gebhard, Freddie, 164
Goodnight, Charles, 76, 85, 87, 88
Goodrich, Benjamin, 35
Goodrich–Laurens Duel, 35
Gould, Helen, 169
Jay, 169
Grayson, Peter, 54
Greeley, Horace, 61
Green, Thomas, 105
Groce, Jared E., 12
Gutierrez–Magee Expedition, 11

H

Halderman, Tom, 146
Hall, Lee, 122, 123, 124
Hanrahan, Jim, 81, 82
Harathzy, Sheriff, 158
Hardie, Shep, 143
Hardin, Barnett, 130
Benjamin, 128
Bob, 131
Callie, 142, 148, 149, 153
Jane (see Bowen), 137, 138, 139, 141, 142, 144, 145, 146, 148, 149, 154
Jeff Davis, 150
Joe, 128, 131, 132, 133, 140, 141
John Wesley, 108, 120, 127–154
John Wesley, Jr., 141, 147, 148, 149, 150, 153
Mary Elizabeth (Dixon), 128, 131
Mattie [see Smith], 154
Molly, 138, 141, 148, 149, 153
Reverend James Gipson, 127, 128, 131
William B., 128
Hardy, Mr. and Mrs., 37
Harrell [Family Ranch], 137
Haynie, Mr., 20, 21
Heard Family, 45
Heard, William Jones Elliot, 45
Heard–Northington Family, 45
Helm, Jack, 138, 139

Henderson, J. Pinckney, 39
Heye, Dick [Saddles], 110, 112
Hickok, Wild Bill, 134, 135, 136
"Hippy," 83
Hogan, William Ransom, 33, 39, 40
Hogg, Jim, 149
Holliday, Mrs., 38
Hornsby Children, 20
Hornsby, Daniel, 26
    Joseph, 26
    Mrs. Sarah (Morrison), 17, 20, 22, 23, 26
    Reuben, 19, 20, 22, 23, 26
Hornsby's Fort, 26
Houlshousen, Clabe, 130
Houston, Margaret (Lea), 35
    Sam, 27, 28, 30, 31, 32, 34, 35, 38, 39, 41, 48, 49, 52, 53, 54, 56, 57, 60, 61, 72, 75, 76
Hubbard, R. B., 142
    Richard B., 125
Huckins, Reverend James, 55, 56
Hunt, Flournoy, 27, 28, 38, 39
    Mary (Henry), 38
    P. B., 87
Hunter, R. H., 31, 32
Hutchinson, William Henry, 143, 144

I

Isa-Tai, 81, 82, 83
Ivy, Jake, 6

J

Jack, Patrick, 7
Jenkins, Sam, 106
Jennings, N. A., 114
Johnson, Gail Borden, 67
    J. W., 63
    [Mr.], 44
    Philadelphia (Borden), 63
Jones, Anson, 35, 39
    Randal, 4
    W. E., 137, 149

K

Karankawa Indians, 4, 13, 14
Karnes, Dave, 140

Keese, Tom, 106
Kelliheir, Lieutenant, 76
Kellogg, Elizabeth, 72
Kenedy, Mifflin, 113
Kennedy, Gus, 141
King, Mrs. Richard, 111
    Richard, 111, 113, 118, 119, 120, 125
    Sisters, 119
    W. H., 161
Kiowa Indians, 71, 72, 78, 79, 81, 85, 86, 88
Kiowa–Apaches, 81, 88
Kiowa–Comanche Reservation, 80, 89, 92
Ku Klux Klan, 132
Kwahadi Comanches, 73, 74, 78, 79, 80, 81, 82, 84, 86

L

Lackey, John, 136
Lamar, Mirabeau B., 38, 54
Landrum, J. C., 132, 133
Langtry, Edward, 163
    George, 163
    Lillie, 163, 164, 172, 173, 174
Lapham, Moses, 53
Lattimore, Dr. William, 43
Laurens, Mr., 35, 36
Laurens–Goodrich Duel, 35
Lawson, Thomas, 59
Le Breton, Emily Charlotte, 164
Leslie, Frank, 64
Lewis, Callie, 150
    Captain, 150
Lichtenstein, Sol, 110
Lipan Apaches, 70
Lone Wolf, Chief, 86
Long, James, 11
    Jane, 47
Longley, Bill, 132

M

Mackenzie, Randall, 79, 84, 85, 86, 87
Maher, 171
Mann, Jim, 143, 144

Marshall, 27
Pamelia, 27–40
Mansion House, 32–40
Marcy, Randolph B., 75
Marsele, Pete, 114
Martin, Wylie, 31
Masterson, Bat, 82
McClure, John, 109
McCulloch, Ben, 147
McDowell, Henry, 47
McFarlane, Robert, 62
McGovern, 108
McKay, 108
McKinstry, Judge, 52
McNelly, (Rebel), 114, 125
Carrie, 113, 114, 115, 125
Leander H. (Lee), 103–125
Mary Downey, 103
P. J., 103
McNellys, ["Little McNellys"],
   108
Meader, Marshall, 123
Menard, Michel, 54, 55
Menefee, Thomas, 45
Mercer, Eli, 44, 45, 50
Penelope [see Borden]
(Penelope Borden's Sister),
   55
Mexia, Jose Antonio, 8
Milbank, Jeremiah, 64, 65
Milburn, Elizabeth [see Bailey],
   5
Miller, James "Killin' Jim," 150
Mrs. James, (nee Clements),
   150
Milton, Jeff, 151
Mina, Francisco Xavier, 11
Miner, Darius, 63
Minna-a-ton-cha, 91
Monroe, N. W., 160
Moore and Smith Publishers,
   153
Moore, Dr., 90
Francis, Jr., 53
Morgan [Family], 130
Morgan, J. B., 138
Morose, Helen Beulah, 151, 152
Martin, 151, 152, 153
Muldoon, Mr., 14

Munson, Joe, 10
Mordello, 10
Robert, 10
Murietta, Joaquin, 159

N

Nacona, Chief Peta, 74, 75, 76,
   78, 93
Neal, [Ranger], 25
Neighbors, Robert, 75
Neptune, 55
Nicholson, Stephen, 4
Nixon, L. S., 73
Noakes, Martha, 110
Tom, 110
Nokoni Comanches, 74
Northington–Heard family, 45
Northington, Anita, 45
Elizabeth, 45
George III, 45
Mentor, 45

O

O'Brien, Pat, 167
Oglesby, Captain, 161
"Old Three Hundred," 3, 11, 44
O'Quinn, Ruff, 78
O'Rourke, Paddy, 162, 163

P

Pa-ha-u-ka, Chief, 75
Paramoor, Green, 136
Parker, Baldwin Jr., 96
Benjamin, 71
Cora [see Shaw]
Cynthia Ann, 68–96
Cynthia, 90
Daniel, 69, 96
Gaily Faith [see Davis]
Isaac, 75, 77
James, 69, 70, 71, 72
(Elder) John, 68, 69, 71, 95
John, 68, 72, 73, 88
Laura Neda, 94
Lucy Duty, 68
Neda, [see Birdsong], 95
Pecos, (Peanut), 74, 78
Prairie Flower, 74, 76, 77,
   78, 94

Quanah, 68–96
Sally White, 68, 71
Silas, Jr., 78
Silas, 68, 69, 70, 71, 72, 88
White, 93
Penateka Comanches, 81
Perdue, A. J., 143
Perry, James F., 47, 52
Perserverance, The, 54
Pinole, [Comanche food], 58
Placido, Chief, 75
Pleasants, H. Clay, 122, 123, 124
Plummer, James Pratt, 72, 73
L. M. S., 71
Rachel, 71, 72, 73
Polley, Mary [see Bailey], 5
Potter, Colonel, 117
Powell, Peter, 11

R

Rabb, Andrew, 12
Raguet, Anna, 34
Randlett, Captain, 117
Raymond, Mrs. N. C., 77
Reagin, Dick, 137
Reynolds, Peter, 4
Rice–Rittenhouse Hotel, 39
Roberts, Willis, 54
Robertson's Colony, 28
Robertson, Sterling C., 27, 49
Robinson, Lieutenant, 114, 122
Robles, Carlos, 166
Roe, Mr., 145
Rogers, Joseph, 23
Rohrer, Conrad, 30, 31, 32
Roosevelt, Theodore, 92
Rose, Victor M., 75
Ross, Sul, 75, 76, 77, 93
Rowe, Horace, 108
Rudd [Ranger], 108
Runaway Scrape, 27, 28
Rusk, Thomas J., 34, 38, 39
Russell, William J., 7

S

San Jacinto Day Ball, [First], 34
Sandoval, Jesus (Casuse), 110, 111, 116, 120
Santa Anna, 8, 31, 50
Sargent, John S., 164
Scarborough, George, 151, 153
Selman, John Jr., 151, 152
John Sr., 151, 152, 153
Shadler, Ike, 81, 82, 83
Shorty, 81, 82, 83
Shaw, Cora (Parker), 96
Shazo, Thomas E. de, 95
Sheridan, Phil, 80
Sibley, H. H., 105
Sitterlee, Joe, 123, 124
Slaughter, Gabe, 139, 140
Smith Medium Hand Press, 47, 49, 50
Smith, Ashbel, 34, 35, 36, 38, 58, 59, 60, 61, 62, 63, 67
Benjamin Fort, 32, 33
Berry (Sonny), 108, 112
Dad, 108
"Aunt Mattie," (nee Hardin), 154
Sonnichsen, C. L., 153, 154
Sparks, S. F., 32
Spellman, Elmer, 154
Mrs. Elmer, 154
Standifer, Mr., 20, 21
Stanley, Marcus Cicero, 36
Stearns, Augusta, [Borden], 57
Steele, William, 109, 124, 142
Stephens, John, 94
Stiff, Edward, 36
Stokes, John, 133
Stripling, Raiford, 95
Strother, Mr., 20, 21, 23
Stuart, Dan, 170, 171
Sturm, J. J., 86
Sublet, Phil, 137
Sullivan [Ranger], 25
Sumner, E. V., 59
Sutton Family, 123, 124
Sutton Party, 138
Sutton, Bill, 107, 139, 140
Mrs. Bill, 140
William, 138
Sutton–Taylor Feud, 107, 124, 138, 154
Swain, Harry, 141

J. H. [aka], 141, 142
Swift, A., 63
    Philadelphia [Borden], 63

T

Tafoya, Jose Piedad, 84, 85
Tawakoni Indians, 13
Taylor, Bill, 138
    Billy, 140
    Buck, 138
    Charlie, 138
    Creek, 138
    Jim, 107, 138, 139, 140
    Pitkin, 138
    Zachary, 158
Taylor–Sutton Feud, 107, 138
Tennelle, George, 139
Tenth Cavalry, 83
Teran, Jose Mier y, 6
Texian Emigrant (1840), 36
Thomas, Ann Raney, 9, 10
    John, 9
Thompson, Ben, 122
Tonkawa Indians, 75
Topsannah, 74
Torres, Jesus, 165
Travis, William Barret, 7, 51
Trent, Mrs., 171
"Twin Sisters," [Cannons], 28

U

Ugartechea, Domingo de, 6, 7, 8
Upshaw, Mr., 171

V

Vale, Sheriff, 121
Varner, Martin, 3
Viesca, Augustin, 47
    Jose, 4

W

Waco Indians, 13
Waggoner, W. T., 89
Walker, William R., 154
Watson, [Family Ranch], 137
Webb, Charles, 108, 140, 144, 145
    Walter Prescott, 106
Wharton, William H., 7
Wheeler, Philadelphia [see Borden], 41
"Which Way Tree," 31
White, W. C., 47
Wilbarger, Harvey, 25
    John, 19
    John L., 25
    John Wesley, 17, 19, 25
    Josiah, 17–26
    Margaret (Baker), [see Chambers], 19
    Mathias, 19, 25
Wilde, Oscar, 164
Williams, Annie, 151
    Leonard, 74
    Mr. [aka], 142
    Mrs., 14
    Roger, 41
    Samuel M., 47, 52
Wilson, Charlie, 162
Woll, Adrian, 56
Woodward, Demis, [see Borden]

Y

Yellow Bear, Chief, 90
Yellowstone, The, [Steamboat], 31

187